*Beginner's Guide to*

*Home Coarse Tackle Making*

# Beginner's Guide to
# Home Coarse Tackle Making

LEONARD F. G. BURRELL

PELHAM BOOKS

First published in Great Britain by PELHAM BOOKS LTD
52 Bedford Square, London, W.C.1
MARCH 1972
SECOND IMPRESSION JULY 1976

ISBN 0 7207 0548 7

Printed in Great Britain by
Hollen Street Press at Slough
and bound by Dorstel Press at Harlow

# Contents

# Introduction

Angling becomes more popular every day, attracting to its ranks an ever greater variety of people. Many of them will already be 'do it yourself' minded and will find little difficulty in designing and making their own tackle.

There will still be a large number of anglers who have never used simple woodworking tools, and have little knowledge of what materials to use, but would get great pleasure from catching fish with tackle made with their own hands.

It is for just such anglers as these that this book has been written. An attempt has been made to describe the use of simple tools and basic materials in an easy to understand manner. Step-by-step instructions and diagrams should make the construction of any article in the book simple—even for a complete novice.

Many fishing papers, magazines and books suggest that certain items of tackle can be made by the angler at home, but either assume a certain amount of prior knowledge of tools and materials, or do not state how, in simple enough terms.

Although the book is primarily intended to encourage the complete beginner in home tackle making, it is hoped it will spark off new ideas in those anglers who have been doing it for years.

If you feel 'I've never been any good at making things', don't give it another thought. Have a go; you never know what you can do until you try.

# CHAPTER ONE

# *Materials and techniques*

There are certain basic tools which are essential in order to make even the simplest float or gadget.

An illustration of these is shown in Figure 2 (page 16), plus a few others that make all items easier to manufacture.

Figure 3 (page 19) shows the additional tools which can be borrowed or bought, to widen the scope of the work and enable you to produce professional results with all the items in the book.

## ADHESIVES, MATERIALS AND FINISHES

My wife accuses me of being a bit of a magpie, and I suppose I cannot object to the description.

There is a tendency in my nature to hoard things which most other normal people throw away. But then, this is the way I collect a lot of useful items for gadget making.

The brass strips from old batteries, old pieces of clear plastic from packaging of various sorts, and one wonderful source of supply is children's cheap plastic toys. Innumerable bits of tube, domes, wire and strip all come from toys, mostly from Hong Kong, which have broken rapidly when played with and then get thrown away.

Look at them before they go in the dustbin, and remove any part that appears as if it may have some future use. I have several large tin boxes in my workshop; one contains bits of plastic, one wire and sleeving of various sorts, and another brass strip, bolts, nuts, etc.

One old quiz game that the children had grown too old for produced six bulb holders, umpteen pieces of copper strip and wire, and a useful battery box complete with retaining spring and lid.

So my advice is, even if you have to do it secretly, become a 'magpie', and you can save yourself quite a bit of money if you intend making some of the gadgets in this book.

ADHESIVES

Four main types of adhesives are mentioned in the book; each has its own special use and advantages. In every case, however, it is essential to work strictly to the manufacturer's instructions. This is particularly important with two-part adhesives, since they have to be kept completely separate until you are ready to use them. Any contamination of one with the other will cause hardening to take place. The result will be a useless adhesive.

Let us look at each adhesive in turn and the sort of use to which it can be put.

*Evo-stick or similar impact adhesive:* Usually petroleum-based and obtainable in tubes and two-sized tins. Even when opened the adhesive stays usable for many months as long as the cap or lid is replaced every time it is used.

It will stick plastic, leather, rubber, fabrics etc., to plastic, wood, metal, plaster etc. One advantage that it has, is the speed with which a strong joint can be made. The only disadvantage is that the two parts must be placed together in exactly the right position in relation to each other, as once contact is made, the position cannot be altered.

*Araldite:* A two-part adhesive with a relatively slow setting time but producing a very strong joint. It will stick almost everything to everything else, except for soft plastic of the alkathene or polythene type.

Heat from a boiler or radiator will speed the setting time, but about twenty-four hours is necessary to ensure a really hard joint. It will even stick metal to metal, but does not act as a conductor so cannot be used for electrical connections. A two-tube pack will last for months.

*Plastic Padding:* Again a two-part adhesive used where a quick joint is required. It sets in about fifteen minutes, but the setting time can be lengthened if less hardener is used.

It is very useful for filling holes to seal other materials in, and can be shaped and finished as soon as it is set. A two-tube pack will last for months.

*Balsa cement:* Sold in two main sizes of tubes in model shops. Its principal use is for joining balsa wood. A very quick joint can be made, the cement taking about fifteen minutes to set.

For a butt joint as in the pike float, a cramp or weights should be used to ensure a tight joint.

## MATERIALS

*Aluminium pipe and sheet:* As well as the shops shown in the table there are some retailers who specialise in aluminium sheets and sections.

*Balsa wood:* This is a natural timber growing in South Africa and is very light, soft and easy to cut with simple tools. Obtainable from most model shops in sheets from $\frac{1}{32}''$ up to $\frac{1}{2}''$ thick and usually 3′ 0″ long by 3″ or 4″ wide. Blocks from $\frac{1}{32}''$ up to 3″ square by 3′ 0″ long.

11

MATERIALS AND WHERE TO OBTAIN THEM

| | BICYCLE DEALERS | BOAT BUILDERS | BUILDERS MERCHANTS | CAR ACCESSORY SHOPS | DECORATING SHOPS | DO-IT-YOURSELF SHOPS | GARDEN SUPPLIES | HOBBY SHOPS | IRONMONGERS | MODEL SHOPS | PLUMBERS | RADIO & T.V. DEALERS | SHIP' CHANDLERS | TIMBER MERCHANTS |
|---|---|---|---|---|---|---|---|---|---|---|---|---|---|---|
| ADHESIVES | | * | | | * | * | | * | * | * | | | | |
| ALUMINIUM PIPE AND SHEET | | * | | | | * | | * | | | | | | |
| BALSA WOOD | | | | | | | | * | | * | | | | |
| BAMBOO CANE | | | | | | * | * | | * | | | | | |
| CLEAR PLASTIC SHEET | | | * | * | | * | | | | | | | | |
| HARDWOOD DOWEL | | | | | * | * | | * | * | * | | | | |
| PLASTIC SLEEVING | | | | | | | | | | | | * | | |
| PLYWOOD-EXTERIOR QUALITY | | * | | | | | | * | | | | | * | * |
| POLYTHENE PIPE | | * | | | | | | | | | * | | * | |
| RADIO PLUGS AND SOCKETS | | | | | | | | * | | * | | | | |
| SHEET LEAD AND LEAD WOOL | | * | | | | | | | | | * | | | |
| TERRY CLIPS | * | * | | | * | * | | * | * | | | | | |
| VALVE RUBBER | | | | | | | | | * | | | | | |
| WIRE (COPPER) | | | | | | | | | | | | * | | |
| WIRE (PIANO) | | | | | | | | | | * | | | | |
| PAINTS AND VARNISHES | | * | | | * | * | | * | * | * | | | | |

*Figure 1*

*Bamboo cane:* Any garden supplies shop or ironmongers sells cane in anything from 3′ 0″ to 6′ 0″ lengths. One cane will supply sufficient material for a lifetime of floatmaking.

*Clear plastic sheet:* Obtainable from ironmongers, builders' merchants etc. Usually sold for double glazing, but another suitable material is sold by motor accessory shops for use as side screens etc., on motor cycle sidecars and sports cars.

Usually it is sold by the foot or yard up to 36″ wide. A suitable thickness is 0·02″.

*Hardwood dowel:* Usually made from beechwood, it is sold in 3′ 0″ lengths in diameters from ⅜″ to 1″. The cost per length is negligible and four lengths of varied diameter will provide more than sufficient material for the items in the book which require it.

*Plastic sleeving:* Most radio spares shops sell sleeving in several diameters, available by the yard. Two yards will last for years.

*Plywood—Exterior quality:* Although exterior quality plywood is the most resistant to dampness, any type of plywood is suitable as long as it is protected with paint and varnish.

*Polythene pipe:* Builders' merchants and plumbers are about the only source for this material and some may be willing to supply short lengths.

However, suitable lengths of polythene or alkathene can be cut out of old kitchen equipment like buckets, bowls, sink mats etc.

*Radio plugs and sockets:* There are several different types of plugs but the type shown in the illustrations in the book are the simplest and easiest to use.

*Sheet lead and lead wool:* Keep your eyes open when the roof is being put on a house. If lead is being used for the water-proof flashings the plumber may be willing to give you the offcuts which otherwise will only be left as rubbish.

Another source, but for lead pipe this time, is when some-one is having new sanitary fittings installed. The old pipes are only scrap to the plumber and he may be quite willing to let you have them.

Otherwise it means buying new materials. This costs money and doesn't work any better than the second-hand variety!

*Terry clips:* They are made in a wide variety of sizes and it is wise to take the diameter of whatever you are going to clip to, with you, when you go to buy.

*Valve rubber:* Now that bicycle valves have undergone complete re-design and do not use valve tubing for their seal, valve rubber is becoming increasingly difficult to obtain. This does not matter, however, because soft plastic sleeving and tubing are available in a variety of diameters, and for most purposes it is stronger and better. The small bore tubing is sold by radio spares shops for sleeving, and by aquarium or tropical fish dealers for connecting pumps and filters etc.

*Wire, copper:* This is obtainable from most radio spares shops as enamelled copper wire, but you would probably have to buy a quarter of a pound.

*Wire, piano:* This is sold in model shops as control wire for flying model aircraft, called 'control line wire'. Twenty-five yards will last a lifetime.

Another source of wire is that inside offcuts of electrical cable, or components from old radio or T.V. sets. When the latter are broken up they yield a big assortment of metal sheet, nuts and bolts, wire in various gauges etc., all useful items for gadget making.

Bare copper wire will need insulating sleeving on it if it is to be used for connecting up electrical gear.

Any sort of paint, intended to be used for exterior wood or metal work is good to use, and a coat of polyurethane varnish will even protect just undercoat. Dayglow signal paints are sold by tackle shops, do-it-yourself stores and the manufacturers. Instructions on the tin should be closely followed.

## NOTES ON THE TOOLS
(Figure 2)

*Trimming knife:* Made by Keil Kraft, Swan Morton or Xacto. Spare blades, and blades in varied shapes, are obtainable from most model shops or good ironmongers. The blades illustrated are the most useful ones to purchase.
WARNING: The blades of these knives are usually made from surgical steel and are scalpel sharp. For this reason, to avoid accidents always cut away from you and always keep your fingers BEHIND the blade.

*Backed razor blade:* Ever-Ready, Personna, Gillette. Obtainable from most chemists and barbers.
WARNING: Do not use unbacked blades, other than some makes of single-edged blades. Double-edged blades have an unhappy knack of cutting your fingers without you realising it until you see the blood.

*Glasspaper or sandpaper:* Obtainable from do-it-yourself shops, ironmongers and builders' merchants. They keep most grades, but one sheet of coarse, one of medium and one of fine will make everything in this book.

15

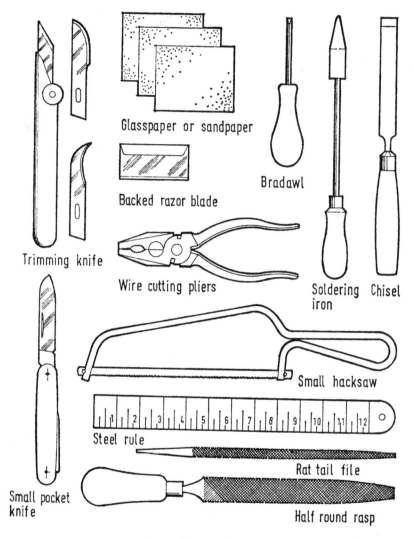

Figure 2

16

*Small hacksaw:* Made by Eclipse and several other manufacturers, and stocked by most tool shops etc. Buy a couple of spare blades as accidents are known to happen. The saw will cut both metal and wood.

*Pliers:* Choose the sort with a long thin nose and a wire cutter on the side. They are not only useful for cutting and bending wire, and holding small parts, but can come into excellent use later for removing hooks from perch, pike and most sea fish.

*Chisels:* Pay a reasonable price for a chisel, since the more you pay, the better and longer it will hold a keen edge.

*12" Steel rule:* Purchase from most tool shops etc. It has a wide variety of uses, from measuring to using as a straight edge for cutting and marking out.

*Rat's tail and half-round rasps:* Most tool shops stock these; the rat's tail version is used for enlarging holes and the half-round for general shaping.

*Small penknife:* The most used tool of all for everything from opening tins to rough-cutting balsa wood. A small one with a single blade is perfectly adequate, so try and avoid one with many other gadgets which you will probably never use—and which don't work too well anyway!

*Soldering iron:* Although an electric soldering iron is desirable, it is not always financially possible to afford one. A simple copper bit, either bought or borrowed, will serve to complete most of the soldering work in the book.

Most good ironmongers and tool shops will be able to supply a medium size copper bit iron. It will, of course, be necessary to have some means of heating the bit—either gas, blow-lamp or primus stove.

*Solder and glue:* The types and uses of these items are explained on pages 10 and 11.

## NOTES ON THE TOOLS
### (Figure 3)

*'G' cramp:* Only a small one is necessary, with, say, a 3″ wide opening, but buy the biggest one you can afford. Better still, buy two—a very small one with, say, 2″ opening, and a larger one.

$\frac{3}{8}$″ *or* $\frac{3}{16}$″ *chisel:* Very useful where small holes or grooves need making or enlarging in wood.

*Small try-square or set-square:* Useful for setting out and checking the squareness of finished work.

*Fretsaw or coping saw:* Once upon a time a fretsaw was the main tool of a hobby called fretwork, examples of which covered everything from models of Westminster Abbey to simple pipe-racks. Now it is the subject of jokes by struggling comedians.

Both tools do a similar job, but the blades of the fretsaw are much finer and available in a greater range of types. However, for any item in the book the coping saw is quite adequate.

Eclipse make a coping saw at a very reasonable price, and it is obtainable in most do-it-yourself or tool shops. Buy a few spare blades, in various grades, save ruining an afternoon when the shops are shut and you have broken your one-and-only blade. A fretsaw is probably more versatile than a coping saw but will be a little more difficult to obtain.

*Electric soldering iron:* The type used for radio work is quite suitable for all items in the book, and is much more

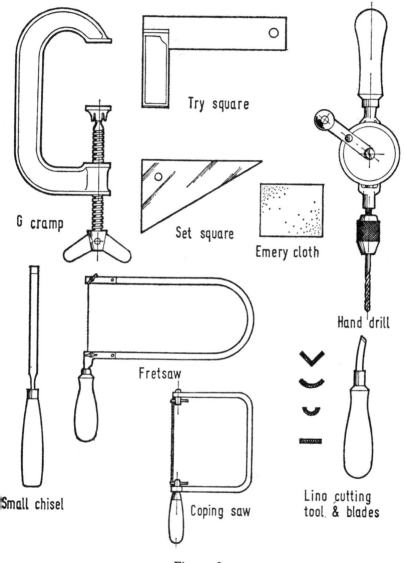

Try square

G cramp

Set square

Emery cloth

Hand drill

Fretsaw

Small chisel

Coping saw

Lino cutting
tool & blades

*Figure 3*

19

convenient for use at home than the old type soldering iron. Obtainable from most electrical dealers.

*Emery cloth:* Most tool shops sell emery cloth which is rather like fine sandpaper. It is intended specifically for cleaning and smoothing metals.

TECHNIQUES

Certain jobs described in the book require a little practice before they can be carried out without thinking. None of them are difficult but as with most things, 'a little practice makes perfect'.

There are also a few minor warnings connected with certain jobs which may not sound very difficult but 'a moment's thought can save a lot of worry'.

*Using sharp tools:* Any elementary book on carpentry and joinery will show you, and tell you how to sharpen simple woodwork tools. They have to be sharp to make the work fun to do, rather than a hardship.

Anything that will cut wood easily will also cut fingers and hands, so bear this in mind. If you have never used carpenter's tools before, start the way you mean to carry on and observe these few simple rules.

1. Keep sharp tools away from children, and do not leave them where they can find them.

2. Always cut *away* from you and keep your holding hand behind the sharp edge at *all* times. It may feel awkward in some instances, but you will get used to it.

3. If the part you are cutting is small, nail a scrap of wood on a small plank and use it to rest the part against. See Figure 4.

4. Make sure you have a first aid box in the house—and that it contains all you need for minor cuts and splinters.

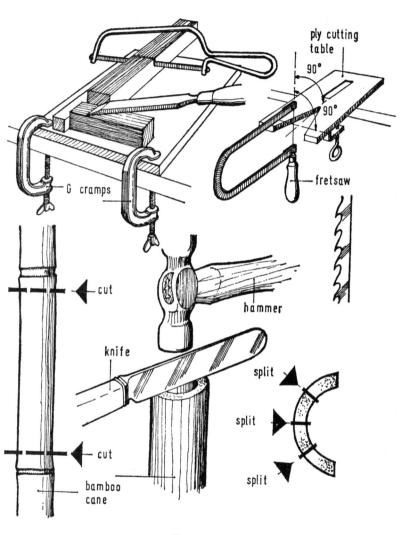

*Figure 4*

*Using a fretsaw:* A fretsaw is a very simple but useful tool if used in the correct way.

Figure 4 shows a simple saw-table that can be made from a small 'G' cramp, and a piece of ⅜" thick ply.

Do make sure when the blade is in the upper and lower clamps, that they are both tight, and that the blade is under some tension.

Do not attempt to force the saw through the wood; a gentle vertical up-and-down movement is all that is necessary and you will find the saw will move through the wood by itself. Remember, keep the blade upright.

Turn the wood, not the saw, and keep cutting while you turn. Even very sharp corners can be formed in this way.

To cut out a hole: drill a small hole first, undo the upper saw clamp and thread the blade through the hole from below. Put the blade back in the clamp, tighten up, and saw around your marks. The waste wood should drop out and the saw can be removed.

Figure 4 shows the way the teeth should be when the blade is in the saw, pointing downwards.

Once again: keep your hands clear of the blade of the saw. It may be very fine but it can saw through 1" of oak, and bones mean nothing to it. I know what I am talking about, I have got the scars to prove it!

*Wood Turning:* Using a small lathe, which forms one of the accessories of most makes of power drill, is good fun. You don't really need one for any item in the book but a more professional touch can be achieved by its use.

If you are tempted to use one please remember these few rules:

1. Do not allow anyone to use the lathe who has not read the manufacturer's instructions about safety.

2. *Always wear goggles at all times.* This also applies to any-one, especially small children, who may be in the room while you are using it.

Stop using it if the visitor will only be in the room for a few minutes.

The 'goggles' bit may sound melodramatic, but a small amount spent on a pair of goggles can save a lifetime of blindness. Fishing is not easy when you are blind!

*Splitting bamboo:* It doesn't sound very difficult to do but this timber is very, very hard and a splinter of it in the finger or hand can be very painful. This is again from personal experience.

The thicker the bamboo strip required, the larger the diameter of cane you must use.

Cut off the length you require between two of the knot rings. See Figure 4.

Take an *old* knife using it as in Figure 4, give the top edge a few taps with a small hammer and the cane will split easily in half. Repeat this on one half section to obtain the size of strip you require.

Figure 4 shows the sort of strips which can be cut in this way.

The bottom half of the thickest garden pea stick will provide as large a strip as you are likely to require for any item in the book.

Do keep your fingers and hands away from the cane while you are splitting it, and do not rub your fingers along its edges until it has been rounded off and smoothed down, the splinters are like needles and very painful if you are on the receiving end!

*Soldering:* A whole book could be filled with soldering technique but a few simple instructions can be put down here to enable the absolute novice to make the few simple connections required in the electrical section.

1. The materials you will require are:
   (a) Cored solder—this is rather like lead wire but has a tiny core of flux running through it.

(b) A small tin of flux suitable for the solder you are using.

2. Heat the soldering iron and clean the copper bit with emery cloth or fine sandpaper and dip it into the flux for a second.

3. Get an old tin lid (the lid of the flux tin will do) and touch the copper bit with solder so that it coats the bit. This is called 'tinning the bit'.

4. Clean the two surfaces to be joined and smear on some flux. Do not do this with your finger; in fact when you clean the surfaces to be joined *do not touch them as grease from your skin will cause oxidisation to take place and the solder will not stick*.

5. Place the pieces to be joined together and hold steady while you touch both of them with the iron. Both coats of solder should run together and the joint be made. Since the solder sets almost immediately no time need be lost in carrying on with the next operation.

See Figure 27c (on page 100), for the method of assembling and holding the pieces for soldering.

Steel, brass and copper can all be soldered but aluminium and its alloys cannot—at least not at home.

There are makes of solder and flux on the market now that will join uncleaned metal parts together. One such make is Wescolite from Gamages, but a chat with your ironmonger or radio spares dealer will solve this one for you.


*Whipping:* This simple little operation plays a large part in most items in the book and is, of course, very useful for repairing fishing rods, when a ring needs replacing.

There is very little that needs saying about it, apart from emphasising that it is important to practise doing it from the diagrams, first of all with fine string and with, say, button thread. See Figure 5.

Keep the turns tight together; this is easy to say but harder to do. It only comes with practice.

Use a round pencil to practise on. Put the initial turns on

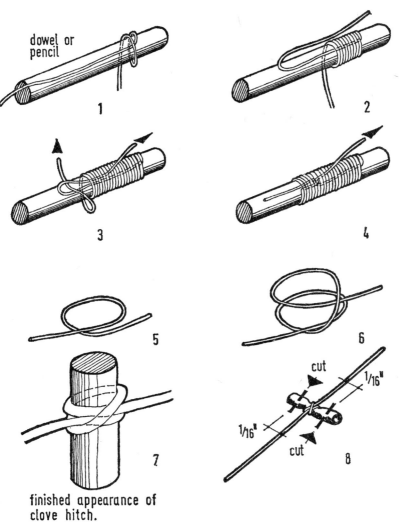

dowel or pencil

1

2

3

4

5

6

7

cut

1/16"

1/16"

cut

8

finished appearance of clove hitch.

*Figure 5*

lightly, holding them in place with your fingers until the turns can be tightened and they grip on the shiny surface. I usually spread a little adhesive on the part being whipped; it does help to hold the turns in place.

*Tying a clove hitch:* This is one technique which is absolutely necessary if the reader intends to use either the sliding float or the pike tackle described later.

Practise it first with a piece of cord and a pencil until you can get it right with your eyes closed.

The method is as follows:

Make a loop underneath the line in the left hand. Then make a second loop on top of the first so that the two parts of the main line lie between the loops. See Figure 5.

Slide the dowel down through the centre of the loops and tighten up the line by pulling both ends. Make sure the loops lie as tightly as possible against each other.

Once you have mastered the knot with cord, try it with fishing line and a piece of a rubber band or plastic sleeving. The heavier and stiffer the line, the more difficult the knot is to tie.

Tie it in the same way, but if you are using rubber for a stop, stretching it, as you tighten up and push the loops together, will help to ensure a good fixing. If you allow the loops to stay apart, the knot will twist the rubber out and the knot will come undone.

A valuable tip, if you are using plastic sleeving as a stop in cold weather, is to warm the plastic with a cigarette end or match. This will soften the plastic so that the line beds itself into the sleeving, and, assuming the loops are close, a firm fixing will result.

Rubber stops need replacing occasionally, since the rubber perishes, but a plastic stop will last as long as the line does.

Once the clove hitch is tight, cut off the ends of the rubber or plastic with a sharp knife on a hard surface. About $\frac{1}{16}$" projection on either side of the line will not slip through a small swivel or the hole through a float, but will pass easily through the rod rings when casting.

Finishing the articles you make is the most important part of the whole operation. Neglect it and what could be a professional looking float can end up as something of an embarrassment.

Before any painting is carried out, it is of utmost importance to ensure that the smoothing down has been done properly. Do not leave rough edges or irregular surfaces, but do use glasspaper, starting with the coarse grade and finishing with the finest. Work on the article until it is smooth to the touch all over; any blemish will show through the paint. Brush off all the dust.

Once you are satisfied, the surface must be sealed to prevent it absorbing the paint and presenting a patchy appearance. This can be achieved with priming paint, or a coat of varnish will effectively seal up the surface. Another sealer which can be used is emulsion paint; its main advantage is that it will normally dry in about four hours in a warm place. Wash emulsion brushes in water as soon as you have finished painting, or they will be ruined.

Wait until the sealer is hard dry, and rub down with fine glasspaper to bring back to a smooth surface again. Now coat the item with the colour chosen, using a matt or undercoat colour with a flat finish. When dry, rub down again and recoat with the same colour. After drying, rub down with worn, fine glasspaper and coat with varnish.

The final result should be professional looking; if it isn't perhaps the following tips will help.

1. Always paint in a dust-free atmosphere and dry where dust cannot settle on the items.

2. Use clean, soft brushes for every coat of paint. Keep two screw-topped jars with turps or white spirit in. The first to

wash off the worst of the paint, and the second to finally clean the brush, wiping the brush on tissues or paint cloth between each wash.

If you want really clean brushes, wash them finally in warm water with soap, and this will remove any remaining paint.

3. Dust off after every rubbing down. A cloth dampened with turps will remove most traces of dust.

4. If the paint or varnish you are about to use has a skin formed on the top of it, remove it and stir thoroughly; it is also likely that the paint will need straining.

Strain the paint through a nylon stocking by stretching the stocking over the paint tin and pouring the paint through the stocking into a clean tin.

A wise move is to keep a few small jars or tins so that, when a larger tin is half full or less, and a skin has formed, it can be strained into a smaller container. This removes the cause of the skinning—the air inside the larger can.

5. Although glasspaper is quite effective for rubbing down paint, a much quicker and efficient method is with wet-and-dry waterproof paper. Glasspaper does tend to clog up with paint whereas wet-and-dry does not, and it produces a very flat surface quickly.

Choice of paints is wide, but for the home handyman, Messrs. Humbrol of Hull make a range of paints in small tinlets which provide ample paint for many accessories. They also make Dayglow signal colours for the tops of floats etc., and these can normally be obtained from good angling shops. Avoid varnishing Dayglow colours as it does tend to lessen their effectiveness and is not really necessary, since the colour is glossy itself and stands up well to wear and tear.

# CHAPTER TWO

# Float making

Floats have always been a source of temptation to the angler and always will be. He enters a tackle shop to buy a few pence worth of maggots and leaves with twenty pence worth of floats, which just happened to take his fancy. He didn't really need them, but those shapes, those colours—a temptation he could not resist.

One snaggy weed bed, or a good fish and a weak line, and expensive and favourite floats are quickly lost.

Now is your chance to avoid these temptations and irritations—in two evenings you can make yourself enough floats to last several seasons.

They are just as efficient as those from the tackle shop and you can make them just as colourful and, with a little practice and patience, equally professional looking.

Let's start by describing how to make the simplest possible float of all.

## QUILL FLOATS

**MATERIALS**

Feathers from any species of large birds e.g. seagulls, swans, geese, crows, etc. Such feathers can be found in large numbers

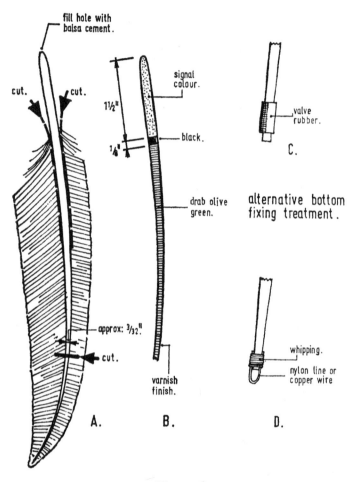

*Figure 6*

30

on most beaches or in fields. Collect a few whenever you visit likely spots and store them for later use.

## CONSTRUCTION

Figure 6A shows the first step. Remove the plume from the quill in the direction of the arrows with a sharp razor blade or modelling knife. Any remaining pieces of plume can be removed with fine sandpaper.

Do not attempt to remove the plume in the opposite direction, if you do you will risk cutting into the quill and ruining its natural buoyancy.

Cut off the thin end of the quill so as to leave at least $\frac{3}{32}$nd of an inch of quill diameter (about the thickness of a matchstick). This is about the minimum for adequate strength.

Since the root of the quill (the thick end) is to be the top of the float, the hole that is normally there needs to be filled with balsa cement, and allowed to harden.

Figure 6B indicates a suggested colour scheme which shows up well on most waters, the signal colour being a personal choice. Red, orange and yellow are best for daylight and white or yellow for torch illumination at night.

The lower section of the float is best painted a dull green or brown, to make the section below water as inconspicuous as possible. The black band helps with visibility, particularly at any distance and adds a little professional touch.

Painting quills is very simple and since no priming is required, after light sandpapering, matt colours can be applied direct, a final glossy finish being given with a coat of clear varnish.

Fit the finished float with a short length of valve rubber when it is dry as at 6C, and add a rubber float ring if two line fixings are required.

Incidentally, float rings are easily made from the insulation covering to flexes and cables of various diameters. Cut around the flex to the wire core about 2" from the end, slip the cutters on a pair of pliers into the cut and pull off the outer insulation. Chop this piece up into $\frac{1}{16}$" lengths and you will have enough rings for approximately thirty floats.

If you prefer a bottom ring on your float, Figure 6D shows how it should be done. Do it before you paint, and smear the tip of the float with balsa cement before and after whipping. This will ensure a firm anchorage.

If nylon line is to be used, a good fixing will be ensured if the .ends of the nylon are crimped with pliers before whipping, otherwise it may tend to slide.

Simple whipping is described in Chapter 1.

*Colouring quills and line with dye:* Painted quill floats do tend to chip after prolonged use which is a little unattractive. A more permanent finish can be imparted to the float by dyeing it, prior to painting, with a dye used for man-made fibres.

Nylon is one such product and experimenting, using as concentrated a solution as possible, will give the correct soakage time for the intensity of colour required.

Dark greens and browns are best for floats, and manufacturers' instructions should be adhered to regarding the temperature of the dye to give best results.

Nylon or monofilament line can also be dyed in similar fashion. This is best done prior to winding on the reel spool, needless to say. An even colour is easier to attain if the line is wound on a piece of firewood, enabling the dye to get to every part.

*Coloured line:* brown or green is less visible to fish when used for ledgering purposes.


## SMALL BALSA AND BAMBOO FLOATS

Small floats up to about 6" long with balsa bodies can be quickly made and look extremely professional when finished. The design is a matter of personal preference and many ideas

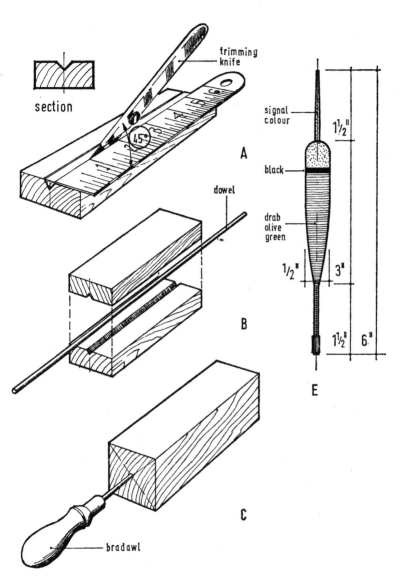

*Figure 7*

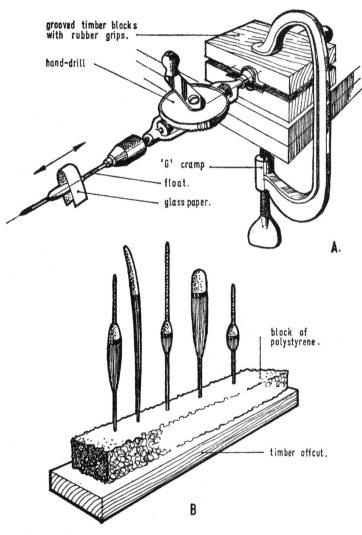

grooved timber blocks with rubber grips.

hand-drill

'G' cramp

float.

glass paper.

A.

block of polystyrene.

timber offcut.

B

*Figure 8*

can be gained by having a look in the tackle shop window, or browsing through a catalogue. But why not be original and design one yourself.

## MATERIALS

Slithers of cane about match-stick size in section and of a length to suit overall length of float.

Two strips of balsa $\frac{1}{2}'' \times \frac{1}{4}'' \times$ length to suit float body.

Copper wire or heavy nylon line for bottom loop if required.

## CONSTRUCTION

Using a trimming knife, or backed razor blade and a steel ruler, cut at an angle and make the 'V' groove down the centre of one side of each half. See Figure 7A section. The cane slither can be rounded by twirling it inside a folded piece of sandpaper and moving it in and out at the same time. Put a rounded point on the top and taper the bottom down a little.

Try the cane in position as illustrated in exploded diagram B. If the two halves of balsa will not close properly enlarge the bottom of the V groove using a folded piece of sandpaper. See Figure 9A.

When a good fit has been obtained glue the two halves together in the correct position on the cane, using balsa cement.

An alternative method of construction is to use a piece of square section balsa. Mark diagonals across each end of the block to find the centres and drill carefully in from both ends (7C), using a sharp bradawl or $\frac{1}{8}''$ drill.

The block can be glued on to the bamboo spine as before.

When the cement has set, shape up the balsa body to rough section as in Figure 9D. Keep shaping the corners of the body off until a reasonably round shape is attained.

The body may now either be finished off by twirling the float inside folded glasspaper or by setting up the hand lathe shown in Figure 8A.

In order not to damage the bamboo stem and to give sufficient extra length to fit into the drill chuck, allow an extra $\frac{1}{2}"-\frac{3}{4}"$ when making the stem.

The sketch shows the drill fixed to the edge of a table with a 'G' cramp, but it could of course be held in a bench vice.

Carefully used, glasspaper wrapped around the float body while the drill is turned by the free hand, will bring a fine, round finish to the float body.

It is easier if a willing assistant can be found to turn the drill; this leaves both your hands free to use the glasspaper, and support the other end of the float.

Whichever method you choose to finish your floats, use a very fine grade of glasspaper last of all. This will impart a really smooth base for painting and help to get that desired professional finish.

If you like an end ring, now is the time to whip one on; if not, and you intend to bottom fix the float to the line with valve rubber, drying the painted float can be a bit of a problem. With an end ring it is easy; a short length of wire or cotton tied to the ring enables it to be suspended from a line or length of wood to dry.

Let's assume that you have allowed a little extra length on the float stem to fix it into the drill chuck when glasspapering. Don't cut this off yet, as it will serve to support the float during the painting process. A useful stand can be made from an offcut of polystyrene glued to a block of wood. The extra stem length can be easily pushed into the stand and will hold it sufficiently for painting. See Figure 8B.

Coat the whole float with white priming, and allow to dry hard. Sand down with fine glasspaper. The lower half of the float can be painted a drab green or brown, and the upper half with white undercoat as a base for the signal colour. When dry, glasspaper with worn fine glasspaper. Application of the signal colour comes next and manufacturers' instructions regarding flowing the colour on generously should be observed for best results. When dry, follow with the black bands, again using matt colour. It may take a little practice to get the bands to look crisp and neat but persevere; try holding the brush still and twirling the float quickly against it.

Finally varnish all over with clear polyurethane varnish and allow to dry.


## PIKE FLOAT AND PILOT

Figure 9 shows a pike fishing float (for live or dead baiting) of a type that supersedes the fixed variety.

This type enables the angler to strike through the float and be in direct contact with the fish right away. It also offers much less resistance to a taking pike, its slim bomb-shape sliding easily below the water. A fixed float makes casting with the shorter pike rod very difficult; a sliding float like this makes the job easier and allows much greater accuracy, with the bait finishing at just the right depth. Such floats are also extremely useful for sea pier or harbour wall fishing.

Figures 10A, B and C show details of a suitable pilot float and E illustrates the general arrangement of the complete tackle.


MATERIALS FOR PIKE FLOAT

$1'' \times \frac{1}{2}''$ balsa strips. A small diameter plastic drinking-straw or an empty ballpoint pen refill.


CONSTRUCTION

Since you are making your own floats, why not make, say, three: one 3", one 6" and one 9" long, plus one pilot float. These will cover every size of bait you are ever likely to use.

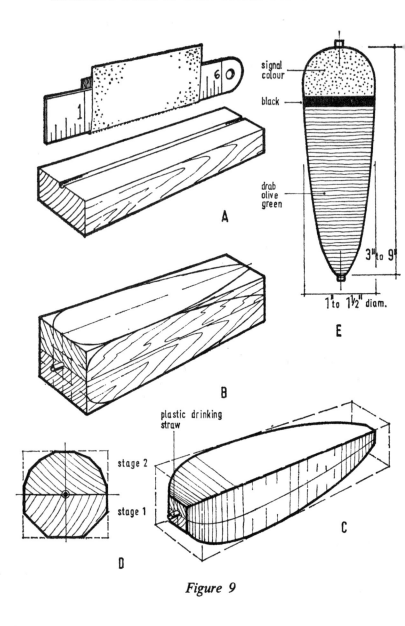

Figure 9

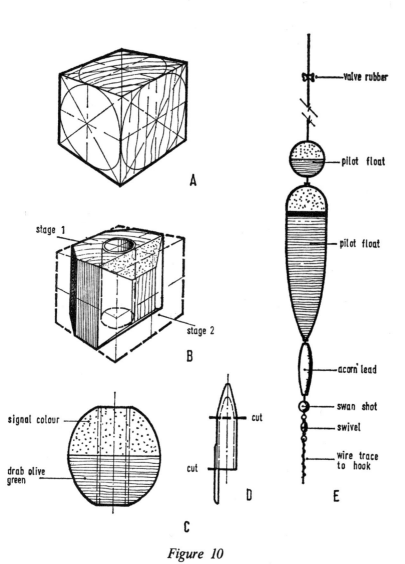

A

stage 1

stage 2

B

signal colour

drab olive
green

C

cut

cut

D

valve rubber

pilot float

pilot float

acorn lead

swan shot

swivel

wire trace
to hook

E

*Figure 10*

Start by cutting off two strips of balsa to the lengths required and mark a centre line down one face of each strip. Wrap a piece of medium sandpaper around a steel ruler and using the edge, rub a groove, half the diameter of the plastic tube, along the line marked on the faces. Figure 4A.

Having cut the plastic slightly longer than required, try it in position between the two halves; widen or deepen the groove until a tight joint is obtained along both edges.

Cement the plastic tube into one half of the float, then cement the second half in place. Hold it together until set with a couple of elastic bands.

When the cement is dry, smooth the four long faces to a level surface. Using a piece of greaseproof and carbon paper, trace off the shape and transfer it to the four faces of the block. See Figure 9B.

Using a sharp chisel or large modelling knife, shape to the first main profile as C.

Take the next step to the final shape in the stages at D, working right along the curve of the float body.

Finish off to a smooth round section by twirling one half at a time inside, first medium, then fine sandpaper.

Prime, paint and varnish, as previously described, to the desired colours.


MATERIALS FOR PILOT FLOAT

The plastic top off a cheap ballpoint pen, or a 1″ length of rigid plastic tube. A 1″ × 1″ × 1″ cube of balsa.


CONSTRUCTION

1″ × 1″ balsa is normally purchased by the foot, so before cutting off sufficient for the float, one job is easier to do with the material uncut. Smooth off one square end of balsa with glasspaper and mark diagonals across to find the centre line.

Measure the outside diameter of the pen top or plastic tube, drill into the centre of balsa 1″ deep, and cut off a 1″ length. Drilling the hole before cutting reduces the chances of splitting the timber.

If a large twist drill is not available, drill a ¼″ diameter hole, cut off the 1″ length and enlarge the hole to accept the tube using a small circular rasp or rat's tail file. Carefully cut off the top of the pen top 1″ long, cement into the balsa with balsa cement and set aside to dry. See Figure 10B.

When dry, roughly shape it with a modelling knife as before, and sand down as spherically as you can.

The reason for using a pen top with an inside diameter of about ⅜″ is to enable the valve rubber float stop to pass through the pilot float.

Finish as previously described.

The finished pike tackle should be mounted as Figure 10E, the stop being made of either a short length of elastic band or a piece of valve rubber tied on the line to set the bait at the desired depth. You will find the knot used to tie the stop described in Chapter 1 on page 25.

## REED FLOATS

MATERIALS
Here is a simple float made from dried reed stems. This type of float is ideal for fishing in reed beds for wily tench and bream or for that matter any species. Varnished naturally with a tiny signal colour top, it is most unobtrusive and blends perfectly naturally.

Gather a few reed tops in March before the spring growth has taken a hold, and if they are not damp they are ready for use.

Figure 11 shows a typical reed length and where to cut it to use as floats. Floats made from reeds are extremely

41

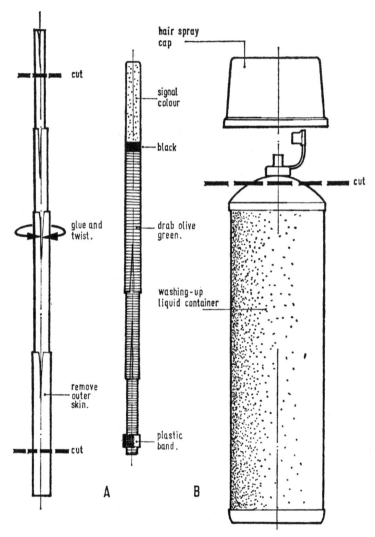

*Figure 11*

42

buoyant, so avoid using sections of reed over $\frac{1}{4}$" diameter and more than, say, 4" long.

Experiments have shown that a 6" length of reed $\frac{1}{8}$" diameter will just cock and show, say, $\frac{1}{2}$" of top with 1 BB shot —ideal for tench close in, in quiet swims.

CONSTRUCTION

Choose a sound length of reed that does not collapse under light pressure across the stem, and cut off the top section that is less than $\frac{1}{8}$" diameter. Cut about 6"–8" off, and peel away the loose outer bark at the thicker end. You may find this will just slide off. Under the bark, just removed, you will find a joint mark similar to that in bamboo, and cut on the waste side of this joint. Very often this will give a solid end to the float but at worst the outer shell is thicker and stronger here, leaving only a very small hole to fill.

Fill such holes with scrap balsa, tapered down with a knife and stuck in with balsa cement.

Spread cement around the top edge of each 'bark step' and down the crack in the bark. By twisting the main stem inside its loose bark skin, inside the fingers, the cement can be spread under the bark, sealing it against water. Set aside to dry.

The way up you intend to use the float does not matter but decide this first if you intend to put a coloured signal top to the float. The float is most natural without colour but if you use the float thickest end up, just put a spot of signal colour on the top end, this is quite visible to the angler but not to the fish.

Use white undercoat under your signal colour as before, and finish by giving the whole thing two coats of polyurethane varnish. See Figure 11A.

Furnish each with float rings on one or both ends, depending on your style, and you have unobtrusive floats for elusive fish. They look smashing when finished, cost nothing for materials, and if you lose six in one season, well there are plenty more reeds by the bank!

## SIMPLE FLOAT CASE

Float cases are not expensive, but most commercial models of the plastic or metal tube variety, are too narrow in diameter to hold more than a few assorted floats. Try to put a fat float in and it jams the rest in the tube. Result: frustration. The case described here costs nothing and takes about a quarter-of-an-hour to make.

MATERIALS

One empty giant economy size plastic washing-up liquid container, approximately 9½″ long by 2½″ diameter.

One plastic cover from a large size hair lacquer or air freshener spray, 2½″ diameter.

CONSTRUCTION

With a sharp knife point, cut off the top of the plastic container as in Figure 11B. Wash the container out to remove any remaining liquid, and when dry fit plastic cover.

Sand between the top and bottom ridges to provide a key. Prime and paint any colour to choice. This makes a float container that will even hold large pike floats.

An alternative finish is a sheet of Contact or similar self-adhesive decorative plastic. Cut it to size and rub it gently down on to the tube with a smooth, round object like a ball-point pen or the back of a comb. A short piece of old broom handle rolled inside the case will give a firm surface to rub against.

## CASTING FIXED FLOATS IN DEEP WATER

Why is it that the most promising still-water swims, particularly in pits, always seem to be deeper than the length of your rod?

Casting with a fixed float into a deep swim was a problem I encountered some years ago. This was a favourite swim which varied from 10' to 12' and had the additional hazard of overhanging trees close behind.

I solved this by evolving a casting method I have never seen described before.

Figure 12 shows the positions of the hands, float and line, just before casting. The most important part of the casting technique is to release the line from the index fingers with the correct timing.

Start the cast either overhead or horizontally, depending on the surrounding undergrowth. When the rod is just overhead, or in the equivalent position sideways, release the lower hook length of line. A split second later, release the line from the reel. The line should fly out reasonably straight without tangles.

It is a good idea to practise this cast without a hook at first, it will prevent a nasty situation arising if you fail to release the line from your left index finger.

This method prevents the hook being magnetically attracted by that small twig in an inaccessible place up that tree behind you. It will also enable you to fish a swim up to 2 feet deeper than the length of your rod in restricted circumstances.


## MAGGOT LAUNCHER

When fishing at some distance out in a lake or river, it is common practice to add to the normal ground bait with a regular feed of maggots.

45

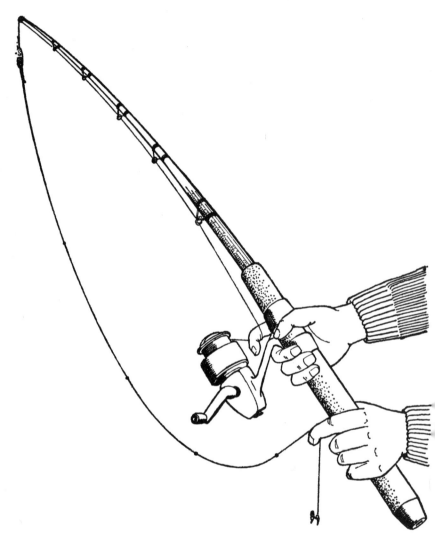

*Figure 12*

There are several ways of getting the maggots to the spot where they are required. In order of inefficiency and disturbance they are:

1. Grab a handful of maggots, stand up and hurl them as hard and as far as one can. They invariably fall short, spread out too far in the wind, and your elbow and shoulder joints soon provide painful reminders of the effort you put into the operation.

2. A swim-feeder works well in rivers, but not so efficiently in lakes, there being no current to empty it, unless it is jerked across the bed of the lake. It makes quite a splash as it goes in and probably makes timid fish very wary.

3. Wrap a handful of maggots in a paper handkerchief along with a stone. Hold the four corners together and tie with a piece of cotton. Hurl this out into the lake to land above the spot you are fishing. In a river, judgement must be made of the speed of the current so that the maggots, carried away by the current as the tissue disintegrates, pass along the swim. Again it is necessary to wave the arm to throw it, and again, there is a splash which increases with the size of the stone and number of maggots used.

4. Use a maggot launcher or catapult with which you can fire maggots with reasonable accuracy from concealment, without disturbing the fish either with waving arms or splashes in the water. The angler may have to make allowance for wind, but this comes with practice. Match anglers and specimen hunters alike use catapults for maggots, and the majority of such catapults are home made. The commercial version seen by the author appears to have one main disadvantage—the pouch is made from two pieces of leather with a tight seam on three sides. Not only is it difficult to grip, but will tend to provide the kind of crack into which the maggot likes to crawl and become trapped.

The version to be described has its pouch lined with a plastic receptacle and leaves no crevices for maggots to enter. It also has an efficient thumb- and finger-grip.

47

MATERIALS

6" × 10" × ⅜" plywood.
2 pieces of ¼" square rubber 14" long.
Whipping thread.
One piece of leather 3½" × 2½".
3 small pieces of hardwood dowel.
1 plastic cup about 1¼" diameter and 1" deep.

*Note:* The leather can come from an old purse or bag, and the plastic cup can be part of a child's soft plastic toy (a doll's feeding bottle, for example). See Figure 13D.

CONSTRUCTION

Mark the centre line of the catapult on the ply and draw the inner and outer circles from one centre, with either a pair of compasses or a simple trammel made from a piece of cardboard about 8" long and 1" wide. Make a small hole for a pin at one end and two holes at the other for a pencil point to go in, spaced apart the width of the ply ring.

The curves where the handle meets the ring and at the end of the handle, can be drawn freehand. Don't forget the two extra internal bumps to accept the rubber.

Drill the two ¼" diameter holes to accept the rubber and one more to pass the saw blade through inside the circle.

Cut the inner shape out first with either fretsaw or coping saw, and then the outside shape as in Figure 13A.

Round and smooth all edges with a rasp and sandpaper, giving particular attention to the inside edges of the two holes for the rubber.

The shape of the leather pouch is best made up by first making a paper pattern to suit the size of the plastic cup available. Allow a little more than necessary for the seams; this can be trimmed down afterwards. Cut the leather pattern out with a sharp trimming knife or razor blade, and stick the hardwood finger-grip in position with Evo-stick, or similar.

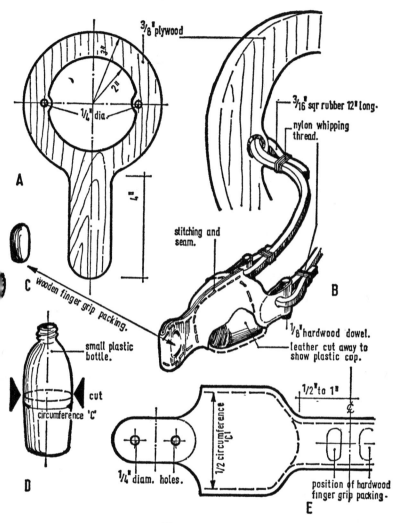

*Figure 13*

49

The two halves of the leather over the finger-grip can also be stuck together, which will make sewing-up easier. See Figure 13.

Try the two dowels, around which the rubber goes, in position. Mark and punch out the holes for the rubber.

A simple punch can be made from a $\frac{1}{4}''$ tube of steel, brass or even copper, if one end has its edge sharpened with a fine file. As a last resort, try using an office paper punch or buy a proper punch from a leather goods shop.

Sew around the whole of the finger-grip and one side of the pouch with strong thread. Use an awl to make the holes and if the needle is hard to push through, use a piece of hardwood to push with, and a pair of pliers to pull.

Glue the plastic cup in with Evo-stick as tight to the sewn edge as possible, and sew up the remainder of the pouch.

The plastic cup must also be sewn in around its open end, as Evo-stick will not secure soft plastic.

Wrap the two tongues which fix to the rubber, over the dowels, so that the holes coincide, and glue together with Evo-stick.

While the manufacture of the leather pouch etc., is in progress it is a good idea to give the ply frame a couple of coats of polyurethane varnish.

Cut the rubber into two equal lengths and pass one end of one piece through the hole in the frame. Get a friend to stretch the two pieces for you, while you whip and tie the connection.

Repeat this at the other side of the frame, keeping the short return ends on opposite sides, and again on the pouch connections.

With a bit of practice, this launcher can be fired without the maggots falling out. Although the author has never found it necessary, a small circle of thin plastic held on with a thread hinge can be made as a light push-in flap to retain the maggots.

The force of firing will burst the flap open and send the maggots on their way.

## ROD RESTS

The average cheaper-type of rod rest available in most tackle shops is not designed or made to suit ledgering. Their main handicap is the lack of clearance at the bottom of the fork for the line to run free. There are some cheap rubber-topped rests which do give line clearance and the angler should watch for these when purchasing.

The best way to ensure that you use a rod rest that gives adequate clearance for the line to run freely under the rod, is to make it for yourself. Two types of rest are described, with several alternative methods of fixing tops to bank sticks.

MATERIALS

$\frac{3}{8}$" plywood of a size suitable for the leads of the rests. Bank sticks of various lengths from $\frac{1}{4}$" mild steel rod, $\frac{1}{2}$" bore aluminium or copper tube, or $\frac{1}{2}$" diameter hardwood dowel.

CONSTRUCTION

Figure 14 shows two types of heads, A and B. A is a general purpose rest which will slip easily into the rod bag and is fairly light to carry. B is the type of rest favoured by the author for night fishing. Painted white it can be seen even without a light, and provides a wide enough surface to avoid the annoying tangle you sometimes get when you miss the rest at night, and the line finds a set of bramble thorns just below it.

Whichever design you choose to make, lay this out on the plywood, starting from the centre line.

Cut the shape out with the fretsaw or coping saw and round off all edges except the bottom, with rasp and sandpaper.

Pay particular attention to obtaining a smooth, rounded finish in the line slot.

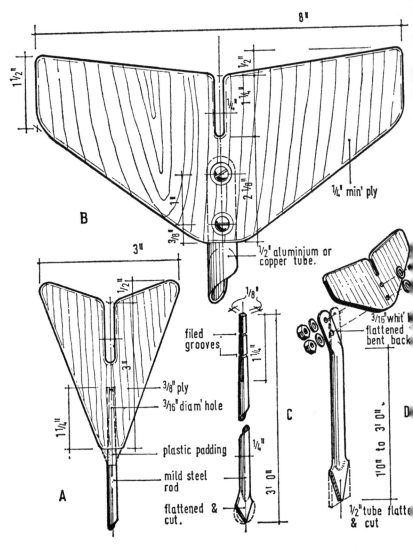

*Figure 14*

For type A, and using a bank stick from $\frac{1}{4}''$ diameter mild steel rod, drill a $\frac{1}{4}''$ diameter hole vertically on the centre line from the bottom. Take care not to split the ply doing it.

Flatten and file the bottom end of the bank stick to a diamond shape and taper the top end, with a file, to a square section.

Make two or three grooves across the flat surfaces to act as a key and glue into the head with Araldite and leave to set. See Figure 14c.

When the glue is really hard, round and smooth off the remaining bottom edges of the ply and smooth for painting.

Remove any rust on the bank stick with a wire brush and sandpaper, and wipe off all dust.

A coat of metal primer/surfacer, as used for cars, is suitable for the stick, and prime and undercoat the ply.

Green is as good a colour as any for the stick and the water side of the rest, with white being used on the angler's side of the rest only.

With the wider type of rest, a tubular aluminium bank stick makes a stronger job, the ply being cut and prepared as before. Bolt the ply to the aluminium with short, round-headed bolts, using a washer under the nut on the aluminium. See Figure 14d.

Alternatively, in a later chapter of this book, Figure 26a and 27b on pages 99 and 100 show another type of connection to a tube. A shaped stub at the bottom of the head of the rest fits into the top of the bank tube which has been flattened evenly on both sides. The head can be secured to the tube with a short, round-headed screw as in Figure 34c.

Not quite as strong or rigid as the earlier types of bank stick, but still serviceable, is one made from hardwood dowel. Cut a suitable flat face on one top side, and drill for two countersunk brass screws. Glue the ply to the dowel with Araldite and screw into the ply. If the points of the screws project, file them down flat. See Figure 34c for a similar idea.

The bank end of the stick should be pointed, but with two flat surfaces. This prevents the rest from turning in use.

One advantage of making one's own rod rests is that they can be made to a length to suit a favourite swim. The author has made a very short, wide rest for ledgering, when the rod tip needs to be sunk below water level.

Any rod rest will do, for the handle end of the rod, but again, the reader may wish to make one to his own size requirements. The patterns here, without line slots, do the job very well.

# CHAPTER THREE

# *Ledgering terminal tackle*

Ledgering is an art in itself, as most experts will tell you. Any reader who has tried, will realise some of the problems this stage of fishing creates. He may not be quite so aware of the advantages.

Ledgering offers the bait to the fish in a most natural manner; there is no vertical fishing line running up to the surface from it, and no bobbing float to cast a shadow. If the line is fine enough or coloured to blend with the bottom, it is more or less invisible.

The slightest movement of the bait is registered at the rod end and when a strike is made, direct contact occurs, since there is a more direct route to the bait.

Float fishing is very enjoyable until that stiff breeze springs up, and it becomes difficult to detect the difference between a bite and movement caused by the wind or ripples on the water. You will continue to catch fish if you ledger in such conditions.

Night fishing is, again, best carried out using ledger tackle. A float, lit by a lamp light will catch fish, but the bigger, wiser fish will keep well away.

We will treat the construction of the tackle for ledgering in two stages. This chapter will deal with terminal tackle only (the part below the water), while Chapter 4 will describe bite detection devices at the rod end of things.

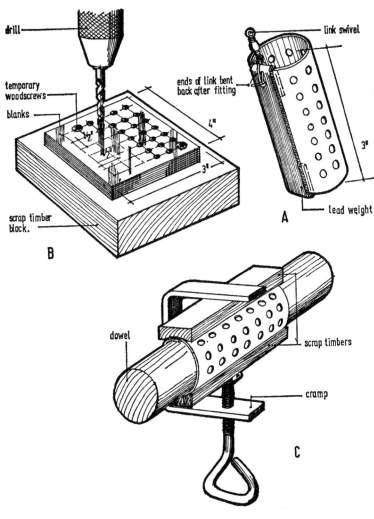

*Figure 15*

## SWIM FEEDERS

The best terminal tackle for ledgering is none at all, just the bait on a hook. Our climate only lets us do this on rare occasions or when we use heavy bait like potatoes and paste for carp on sunken line. The majority of times we are forced to use some method of anchoring our bait at the bottom with a weight. When we fish on gravel bottoms, in streams and rivers, this is easy with proprietary weights which are fairly inexpensive, and since melting and casting lead is a slightly hazardous operation, we won't attempt to make those.

Swim feeders are a different proposition. They are an extension of the ledger weight, serving as a weight and as a container for ground bait to be flushed out by the current or a jerk on the line.

Since they cost in the region of 10p each and have an uncanny knack of becoming lodged into some strange piece of debris in what should be snag-free water, let us see what we can do.

There are two ways of making them:
1. Using 1″ bore thin-walled transparent polythene tube—not easily obtainable.
2. From flat sheets of $\frac{1}{32}$nd gauge polythene and glued up into cylinders. Incidentally, suitable materials are sold for sports-car side-screens or double glazing. There is a third source for the basic tube for quite a serviceable swim feeder. This is the transparent containers for pre-packed screws, nails etc., obtainable from ironmongers and hobby shops. However, these are rather thin, may be brittle and have limited lives.

MATERIALS
1″ bore polythene tubing—transparent and thin-walled. 3″ required per feeder or $\frac{1}{32}$nd gauge transparent plastic sheet, 3″ × 4″ required per feeder.

Strips of 4 lb sheet lead (a few offcuts from a local builders' merchant will make swim feeders for life).

1 largish swivel and link per feeder.

1 small split ring.

### CONSTRUCTION

Let's start by making them from flat sheet. If you intend making more than one, make them all at once; it will save a deal of drilling time.

Using a ruler and sharp point, scratch the lines marking out your 3″ × 4″ squares of plastic and cut them out using a steel ruler and modelling knife or old scissors. Lay them down, one on top of another, in a neat stack on top of a piece of scrap softwood, and either clamp them down with a 'G' clamp or get an assistant to hold them while you drill a $\frac{3}{8}$″ diameter hole at one corner, $\frac{1}{2}$″ in from both edges. See Figure 15B. Having done this, pin the sheets to the softwood with a small woodscrew through the hole. Repeat in the opposite corner and screw down. You are now in a position to mark out a pattern of holes over the whole sheet and drill them out. Remove the screws, lift from the board and smear one top edge and the opposite bottom edge with $\frac{1}{4}$″ wide strips of Evo-stick. Wait about 15 minutes and then wrap the sheet around a broom handle and apply pressure with strips of wood and a 'G' clamp. Repeat this for each one.

Allow a few hours for the adhesive to set hard, then slide the tubes off the broom handle. See Figure 15C.

Flatten out a piece of sheet lead and cut off strips $\frac{1}{4}$″ wide by 4″ long, one for each feeder. If you require a heavier feeder increase the width of the strip or use a heavier gauge of lead sheet.

Bend over $\frac{1}{2}$″ of one end of the strip and slip over the joint in the tube, pinching it on tight with pliers. Now bend the overhanging $\frac{1}{2}$″ at the opposite end into the tube and pinch up tight. Drill a small hole with a bradawl or fine drill $\frac{3}{16}$″ in and on the centre line of the lead strips, to pass through both thicknesses of lead and the plastic tube sandwiched between

With a bit of jiggling the split ring can be forced on to and through the hole in the lead and the link swivel attached. Alternatively, the prongs of the link can be opened with pliers pushed through the hole from both sides and pinched tight.

The method for making the feeders from tube is similar in the last stages but the drilling of holes will have to be done after the tube is slipped on to a piece of broom handle. A good tip here is to plane a flat surface on one side of the broom handle to drill on, otherwise the drill will tend to wander away from where you want the hole.

## GENERAL NOTE ON LEDGER WEIGHTS

Although the standard lead ledger weight, the drilled bullet, the acorn or the Arlesley bomb, all have their purpose, many waters have bottoms which are either weedy or badly silted. Then an alternative type of weight has advantages.

Those about to be described fall into two main classes: stick ledgers which are designed always to stand up straight after burying themselves into bottom weed or silt, and the semi-buoyant type which, although they have ample casting weight in air, will just sink down through water and come to rest gently on weed or silt, keeping swivel and line well above them.

## STICK LEDGERS

**MATERIALS**

Split pieces of bamboo cane about 3″ long (or longer if the bottom you are going to fish has a known depth of silt or weed) and ⅛″ diameter.

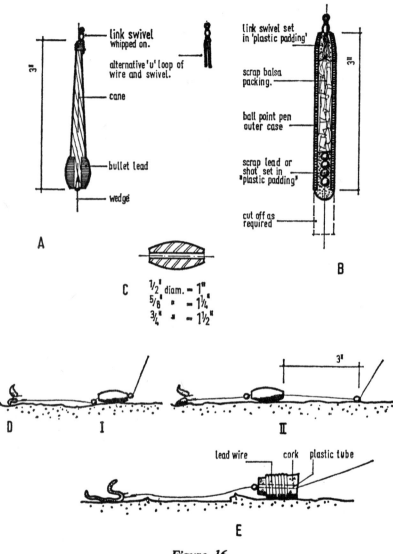

Figure 16

60

Bored lead bullets of preferred weight, or a barrel lead.
One small link swivel per ledger.


CONSTRUCTION

Figure 16A shows the general method.

Round off the cane and taper it towards the top if you prefer it.

Bore out the lead bullet or barrel lead so that the thick end of the cane will be a tight push fit. If you leave a slight shoulder on the cane just above the lead, this will prevent the lead from running up it.

Widen out the bottom end of the bullet slightly, so that the action of glueing and driving a wedge into bottom end of the cane after it is in place, will expand the cane to a tight fit inside the lead.

Slightly split the bottoms of the cane before finally placing in position with Araldite or balsa cement. Force the cane into the hole in the bullet, glue the wedge and drive in place. Trim off the surplus wedge and sand to a smooth finish.

Finally whip the link part of a swivel to the top of the cane, or make a 'u' loop of copper or brass wire as for floats. Pass this through one ring of the swivel before whipping it on. A spot of Araldite or balsa cement will ensure that the loop does not come off in casting and will seal the whipping.

My stick ledgers are painted either matt black or drab olive green, depending on whether I am fishing in black silt or weed.

A coat of polyurethane varnish will give the ledgers a professional finish or they can be left matt, but will then need repainting more often.

## STICK LEDGER FROM A TUBE

**MATERIALS**

One ballpoint pen case.
Scrap balsa or cork.
Some scrap lead or shot.
One link swivel.

**CONSTRUCTION**

Figure 16B shows the general construction.

Remove the small bore ink container from the pen case. Don't throw it away: there are a lot of uses for it elsewhere in this book!

Cut off the end of the pen to a desired length: 3"–4" is usually plenty unless special conditions exist as previously described, when the full length of the pen case should be used.

Cement the link swivel into the tapered end of the pen with Plastic Padding. Pack the pen with pieces of scrap balsa to within ¾" of the bottom, then pack to within ⅛" of the bottom with scrap lead or shots, and finish off with a plug of Plastic Padding.

This latter material can be applied and moulded to the approximate finished shape and then rounded off to a neat finish with glasspaper when dry. Paint as described for stick ledger.

The weight of the ledger can be varied to suit requirements by just reducing or increasing the amount of lead you pack into the end.

## SEMI-BUOYANT LEDGER WEIGHTS

**MATERIALS**

Normally beech dowel rod in short lengths three sizes would be ample, say ¼″, ⅝″ and ¾″.

Balsa could be used if preferred but is far more buoyant and is more liable to damage.

At the end of this section is a description of a ledger made from a small bottle cork, wrapped with lead wire.

**CONSTRUCTION**

As can be seen in Figure 16c this is largely a matter of drilling and shaping. It is best to drill the central small hole first; this gives you a point to shape to at both ends. Make the hole as small as possible—⅛″ diameter is perhaps as small as is practical without the job being too expensive in replacement drills.

Shape the ends down to the torpedo shape with a modelling knife or sharp chisel and finish off by twirling the wood inside a fold of medium, and then finishing off with fine, glass-paper.

Since it is essential to seal the inside of the hole against the effects of water, this is the next step. Paint or cement can be used but I prefer balsa cement. Squirt the tube into the hole and spread with a matchstick or piece of wire.

When dry, paint as previously described, either black, dark green or brown.

When fishing, using the lift method, this type of weight is preferred by some anglers, where casting weight is required but little water resistance.

It should be weighted on either side of the ledger with sufficient shots to sink it just below the water. Figure 16D(i). If used as a float ledger with, say, a sliding float, keep the upper shots 3″ away from the ledger. After tightening there will be sufficient line for the bite to take to give clear indication on the float or detector. See Figure 16D(ii).

Another method of accomplishing the same effect is to use a small, bored, bottle cork. Figure 16E illustrates all that needs to be done.

This has the advantage of being usable as a straight ledger with only one stop weight being required. Paint black or green as preferred.

A small bore plastic tube, or length of wire sleeving, pushed into the cork, will form a clear and friction-free passage for the fishing line.


## BUBBLE FLOAT LEDGER WEIGHTS

MATERIALS
One small bubble float,
Short length of small bore rigid plastic tube or sleeving.


CONSTRUCTION
Figure 17A shows the general arrangement of the finished weight.

Two small holes are bored into the bubble float sides, clear of the filling bungs and exactly opposite each other. The short length of plastic tube is cemented into place, allowing it to project about $\frac{1}{16}''$ on each side. This gives you something to make a fillet of cement around, and ensures a watertight job.

If it is wished, the lugs on the sides can be filed off to give a smoother surface to avoid tangles.

Fill the bubble float with sufficient water to give the desired casting weight, and to make it just sink. Use as a normal bored bullet head.

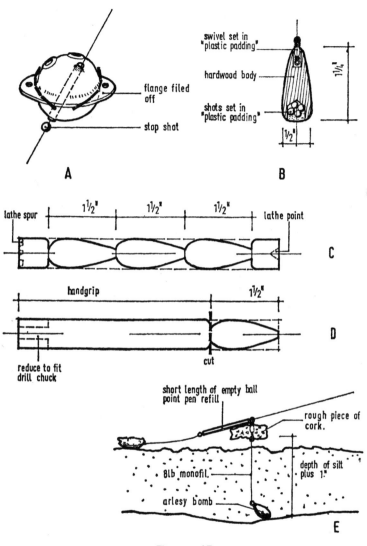

*Figure 17*

## SEMI-BUOYANT ARLESLEY BOMBS

Because its weight in proportion to its volume is so high, the normal lead Arlesley is too heavy for muddy or weedy swims. It tends to sink into the mud and drag the bait after it.

In order to combat this in a similar way to the wooden ledger or bored bubble float, a wooden bomb has the advantage of floating on the top surface of mud and keeping its swivel free to turn in clear water. See Figure 17B.

MATERIALS
One small swivel.
Short lengths of $\frac{1}{2}''$ or $\frac{5}{8}''$ beech dowel.
Assorted lead shot.

CONSTRUCTION
Two methods of construction are open to you depending on whether you possess a small lathe based on an electric drill (Bridges or Black & Decker for example). Otherwise the bombs will have to be made by hand.

*By lathe.* Let's deal with lathe construction first. By experiment it has been found impossible to make more than three at a time on the lathe. The sketch in Figure 17C shows the final stage at which to aim.

Three body blanks are shaped as near as possible to their final shape, leaving them to be cut off with a fine saw.

*By hand.* By hand the process is a little slower and means making one at a time.

Figure 17D shows the final stage and it is suggested that you make each one on a fair length of dowel to give you something to grip. Alternatively, for final finishing off with two or three grades of sandpaper, you can reduce the opposite end of the dowel to a size to fit your hand drill chuck and, with an assistant, so obtain a lathe effect for finishing.

This is similar to the process used in float making, previously described and illustrated in Figure 8A.

FINISHING

Two holes have to be drilled in each ledger body, one about $\frac{3}{32}$" diameter and $\frac{1}{8}$" deep in the small end, and one $\frac{1}{4}$" diameter and $\frac{3}{8}$" deep in the large end. These holes can be drilled without splitting the timber if care is taken. The larger one is drilled more easily if a small size drill is used first, and the drill size gradually increased.

Take a small swivel and, with a pair of pliers, flatten the wire ring at one end, i.e. close it up. Cement this into the small hole with Plastic Padding, taking care not to gum up the free-running of the upper part of the swivel.

Some degree of trial and error is necessary for the next stage, the addition of the weights. Just sufficient weight is required to sink the ledger below water and in the case of the size shown in Figure 17B about four B.B. shot is plenty.

Try this number first, and fill up to a smooth round end with Plastic Padding.

When the padding is dry, usually in about fifteen minutes, sand it all smooth and prime it. Once the priming is dry it can be tested. If it falls down through the water too quickly, either re-drill and omit one B.B. or make another, lighter ledger. I personally make another, because with some baits like bread crust for example, a little extra weight is necessary to sink the bait. Keep the lightest ones for use with maggots or paste.

Finish off with colour to choice. I prefer matt black with a coat of varnish.

## FLOATING SWIVEL

**MATERIALS**
One short length of say 8 lb monofil.
One Arlesey bomb.
One small swivel.
Cork.

**CONSTRUCTION**
This is based on the idea of a small paternoster. The only difference is a small rough piece of cork painted matt black to keep the swivel afloat above the ooze.

Figure 17E illustrates the construction quite clearly. It is really a question of how long should the item be. If you make it more than, say, 3″ you may experience tangles in casting. To help eliminate this I tried adding a short length of black plastic electrical sleeving between swivel and stop shot.

## EXPERIMENTAL LEDGERS

These next two types of ledger weight are not perfect. The experiments I have carried out show they are inclined to be temperamental, but I have caught fish with them.

Short of going down with an aqua-lung and watching the way the weights behave in comparison with standard ones, there is no real way of telling how effective they are.

The aim of these particular designs was to ensure that the swivel through which the line passed was held up clear of, say, 3″–4″ of silt even if the weight was resting on gravel below the silt. Samples from the bottom had shown this silt to be particularly thick.

68

## PUNCH BALL LEDGER (I)

**MATERIALS**
Scrap lead sheet.
One $\frac{3}{4}"$ × No. 6" brass round lead screw.
Short length of valve tubing or plastic sleeving.
One small swivel.

CONSTRUCTION

As the name implies, it is based on the principle of a punch ball, the idea being to produce a ledger which sinks and sits either on the gravel under the silt or on the lower or denser layers of silt. The flexibility of the tubing plus the flat lead bottom tend to reduce the possibility of toppling the ledger over on its side and ensure that the swivel stays clear and free to turn above the mud. Stick ledgers may tend to be pulled under into the silt when the line is tightened.

I have caught big bream using a small version of this idea, so it does work.

Construction is simple: a small lead washer is cut out from scrap sheet lead about $\frac{1}{16}"$ thick and a hole to accept the screw is drilled in its centre. Cover the screw with Araldite and push one end of the tubing over right down to the lead.

Dip one end of the swivel in Araldite and force this into the top end of the tubing to, say, three-quarters of the way up to the centre barrel. Whip the swivel in with nylon thread.

Put aside to set.

Again, to prevent tangles I used a short length of sleeving between swivel and stop shot.

Reversing the shape of the washer would only act as a greater drag on the retrieve and wouldn't improve the performance much.

Figure 18A shows a general view of the ledger in use.

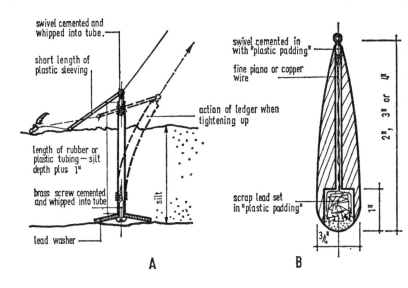

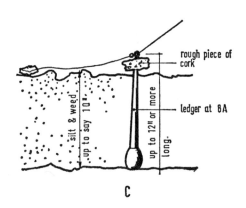

*Figure 18*

70

## PUNCH BALL LEDGER (II)

This is about the most efficient variation of the stick ledger I have. It works well and it does help to catch fish in really bad, silty conditions. The larger varieties are particularly useful when long casting is needed to get at feeding bream well out in a lake.

Some specimen-hunting anglers use one adapted from large bodied floats, weight being added at the bottom and a small swivel whipped on to the top.

The version I am going to describe is intended to work rather like the child's toy with a weighted and rounded bottom, which can't be knocked over. Whichever way it is laid, it always stands up again: This movement ensures that in water the swivel is always on top, poking out above the silt, preventing the hook line and bait from being pulled below the silt and offering least resistance to a taking fish.

MATERIALS

Lengths of square balsa $\frac{1}{2}'' \times \frac{1}{2}''$ or $\frac{3}{4}'' \times \frac{3}{4}''$ depending on size to be made.
Short lengths of copper or stainless cheese wire not thicker than 30 swg. Model aeroplane control line wire will do, as sold in model shops for hand-controlled tethered-flight aircraft.
One small swivel.
Scrap lead or old lead wool, lead shots.

CONSTRUCTION

Three variations of size are shown in Figure 18B; let's make the largest size.

Cut a 4" long length of $\frac{3}{4}''$ square balsa and round it off as described previously for the manufacture of the pike float, and shape to the bomb profile.

Using two or three different sized drills, starting with the smallest size, drill a hole in the bottom about 1″ deep. The average home drill only has a $\frac{1}{4}$″ maximum diameter chuck capacity. The hole should now be increased in diameter to $\frac{1}{2}$″ using a trimming knife or lino cutting gouge. Use special care when the walls are getting thin.

The next step is to drill a small diameter hole from the top pointed end to appear inside the large hole; this is best done with a baiting needle or a straight length of stiff wire.

Lastly, make a small hole about $\frac{1}{8}$″ deep in the top thin end, just big enough to accept the bottom ring and half of the body of the swivel.

Take an 8″ length of fine piano or copper wire and double it in half in the centre. Hook the wire through the top ring of the swivel and thread the wire down through the central hole of the body.

If the small top hole is filled with Plastic Padding or Araldite this will secure the swivel once it is in place.

Using a pair of thin-nosed pliers, bend the projecting ends of the wire back on itself within the hole. When the lead weight is fitted, the wire is permanently fixed and cannot pull out.

My own choice for the lead weight is lead wool. This is used in the building trade for jointing cast-iron pipes and can be obtained from any builders' merchants.

Mix up a quantity of Plastic Padding and line the inside walls and bottom of the large bottom hole with it. The lead wool can now be packed into the hole in layers, adding a little Plastic Padding between each one. The chuck end of a twist drill makes a useful tool for packing. Care should be taken not to pack the lead too tightly on the outer edges. This may split the thin balsa shell.

Pack the edges right up to the top of the hole and finish off to a smooth round end with Plastic Padding. Set aside to dry.

The beauty of using Plastic Padding is the rapidity with

which it sets. After about 30 minutes have elapsed it should be hard enough to sand down to a smooth rounded finish and is ready for painting. My colour choice is black but you could use dark olive green or dark brown depending on which colour you feel is best suited to the water you fish.

A FURTHER IDEA

Although this hasn't been tried yet, it will certainly work and may come in useful for the really bad swim with silt and weed. Also it may appeal to those anglers who like to be really sure that the swivel is standing up out of reach of snags.

Figure 18c shows the principle, although it would only seem necessary where weed is, say, 9" or 10" deep and the stick ledger needs to be about 12" long.

# CHAPTER FOUR

# Ledgering bite detectors

The ideal detecting device for ledgering is nothing at all—just watch the movements of the line either where it lies on the water or where it rests over a ring. This may be excellent for dedicated experts, fishing quietly in private, selected swims, but it does tend to remove some of the excitement from fishing for the average angler, who needs something more than a near-invisible line movement to indicate a bite.

Like nearly all anglers, I like watching the float bob, and disappear. When the weather makes it impossible to float fish, I prefer to use a visible signal of some description, one that is suited to the prevailing conditions and water.

The basic and most important rule in bite detection is that whatever method you use, it must offer the least possible resistance to the taking fish, hence my earlier remark about 'nothing at all being best'. This is where many quite experienced anglers go wrong. You may have seen them, waiting for bites to materialise after a fish has sampled a bait, and felt the weight of a heavy bobbin on the resistance of a badly-made or adjusted proprietary bite detector. The fish leaves the bait and the angler goes home disappointed.

All the detectors in this book have their specific uses, and it is a wise thing not to use one that is too heavy for the type of fishing you intend to do, or for the conditions in which you may be fishing.

## SLIDING FLOAT FITTINGS

For those anglers who insist on using a float where the swim depth is greater than the length of the rod, the sliding float is the obvious answer.

'Use a sliding float' it says in the average fishing book or magazine article. It sounds so easy, but can waste so much precious fishing time and be extremely frustrating.

The ordinary shop-bought quill or cork float cannot be successfully used without an extra side ring being fitted, and even then the chances of it working properly are open to question.

Passing the line through the bottom ring only, the float slides up and down the line beautifully, in the air, but once you have cast it into the water it seems to glue itself to the ledger weight or line and refuse to surface in about nine casts out of ten. Jerking and winding-in seem to have little effect when the float has disappeared.

After it has been retrieved, there is usually no obvious reason why the float refused to surface.

The float fixings described next, eliminate sliding float problems almost completely. The only important thing you must know before tackling up is the depth of the swim, so that the stop can be fitted in the right place on the line.

MATERIALS
Small split rings.
Small swivels.
Various short lengths of valve rubber or plastic sleeving.
Short lengths of aluminium wire (a suitable wire is supplied with several makes of toilet block).
Short pieces of small size rubber bands.

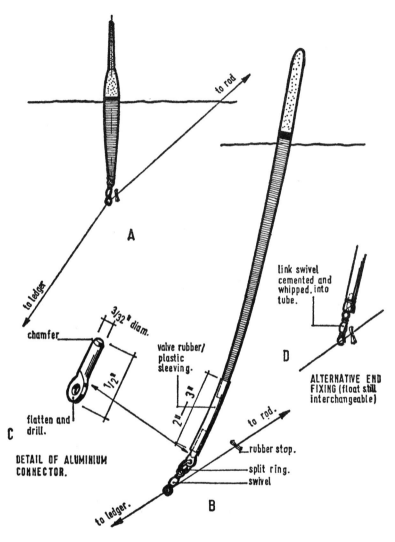

A

to rod

to ledger

C

chamfer

3/32" diam.

1/2"

flatten and drill.

DETAIL OF ALUMINIUM
CONNECTOR.

valve rubber/
plastic
sleeving.

2"

3"

to rod.

rubber stop.

split ring.

swivel

to ledger.

B

link swivel
cemented and
whipped, into
tube.

D

ALTERNATIVE END
FIXING (float still
interchangeable)

*Figure 19*

CONSTRUCTION

A standard shop-bought float can be used as a sliding float, with the addition of just a small split ring and a swivel as in Figure 14A.

Any float will do but the more buoyant the float, the better performance it will put up.

Naturally, with this type of fixing, the float is not readily interchangeable, unless you are prepared to undo a split ring every time.

Figures 14B and c show a method of float attachment which gives interchangeability in a few seconds. It also has the added advantage that, by just removing the float, the angler can change over to ledgering again in seconds.

There are two methods of making the sliding end of the tackle and Figure 19B illustrates the most complicated. This is really only necessary if you intend to use valve rubber, which does perish after a time and is easily replaced on to the aluminium connector.

If you intend to use plastic sleeving it is better to whip the link swivel directly into it. The plastic will virtually last for ever.

Assuming you wish to make the aluminium connector, cut $\frac{1}{2}''$ off the length of wire.

Flatten about $\frac{1}{8}''$ at one end so that it spreads out sufficiently to drill a small hole in to accept the split ring. This can be done with a small drill or a sharp-pointed tool such as an awl. Once a satisfactory hole has been formed, round off the flattened part and file off any sharp edges at the other end as a slight chamfer. Fit the split ring to both connector and swivel.

Next, slide the connector into the end of 2″–3″ of valve rubber, or if plastic sleeving is being used, the end of the sleeving. If held in boiling water or near any heat source for a few minutes, this will make it soft enough to push on.

The other end of the sleeving accepts the bottom of a float, which should have an end small enough to fit into it. Most quills will go in without much trouble. Home-made seagull quill floats are perfect, and I normally use a medium-to-large one myself.

With all the sliding floats described here, it is necessary to be able to clove hitch the rubber band stops into the fishing line. It is suggested that the reader studies the diagrams of the clove hitch in the first chapter on page 25 and practises until he or she can tie one without having to think how. It is very easy once you get the knack. One stop must be fixed about 6"–12" deeper than the depth of water being fished. Too deep and difficulty will be experienced in getting the float to stand up properly. Too short and it is obvious that the float will not appear above the water.

In order to prevent tangles at the hook end of the line, a second rubber stop is necessary about 1' 6" above the weights of ledger. This is clove-hitched into the line as before and (unlike the upper stop which must be trimmed after tying, to a maximum length of $\frac{1}{8}$") can be left as tied, to any length, usually about $\frac{1}{2}$".

Although, after experience, stops can be quickly tied on single-handed, at the start, an assistant to keep the short length of rubber band stretched slightly while you tie the clove hitch, will make the job simpler. Stretching the rubber helps to ensure a tight knot and prevents it falling off after a couple of casts.

Replace the stops occasionally since rubber does tend to perish, and nothing is more frustrating than a float that will not stand up because the stop has gone and you haven't noticed it.


CASTING THE SLIDING FLOAT

The method of using the float is important and follows a set sequence.

1. Cast the float some yards beyond where you want to fish, place the tip of the rod near water level and allow the line to run out until the float surfaces, probably lying on its side.

2. Unless you have previously wiped the line down with a mild detergent, the rod tip will have to be pushed below water level in order to sink the line. A few swift turns on the reel handle will speed this up and probably sink the float again as well. Once the line is sunk, open the baling arm again and making sure the rod rest allows line to run freely, the float will come up and may lay flat again.

3. Carefully turn the reel to close the baling arm, and stand the float up into such a position that the amount of float above water level suits both the distance it is away and your eyesight.

4. A bite will be indicated by a gentle bob, a complete slide under, or by a slow lift to a laying flat position.

Although this sounds a little involved, half-an-hour's perseverance and practice will make you the master of this method of fishing.

Incidentally, the sliding float works very well with one of the stick or semi-buoyant ledger weights.


## GENERAL NOTE ON SWING TIPS

The average commercial swing tip which one buys in the tackle shop, although being suitable for general purposes, suffers from some disadvantages.

1. It offers too much resistance to shy, still-water fish, particularly when the temperature is low (see 2).

2. The flexible portion is usually made of fairly heavy gauge polythene tube, whose flexibility varies with the temperature. The heat of the sun tends to make the tip soft and sloppy. A cold temperature stiffens it up.

3. A fair river current draws the tip out straight and reduces its bite detection effectiveness considerably.

My personal choice is for two swing-tip types. These are selected to suit venue and weather conditions, and their construction is varied to suit any set of circumstances.

By exchanging the valve rubber for fairly stiff nylon line, the still-water swing tip can be stiffened up for use in conditions of surface drift. By using small bore polythene tubing and applying heat to put in a permanent 90° set, a tip for light river currents is to hand. For moderate to heavy currents a much stiffer form of construction gives good results.

## SWING TIPS FOR STILL-WATERS

### MATERIALS

9″ length of bamboo approximately $\frac{3}{32}$″ diameter, or $\frac{3}{32}$″ diameter beech dowel, or broken plastic knitting needle of similar diameter.
Two small safety pins.
Fine whipping twine or thread.
6″ of approximately $\frac{1}{16}$″ bore plastic cable sleeving or valve rubber or P.V.C. tubing, or 25–50 lb breaking strain nylon line.

### CONSTRUCTION

These swing tips are primarily intended for very still conditions on lakes, such as exist in early morning or late evening. They are at their best when used with the finer range of lines, say up to 5 lb breaking strain. If a breeze is evident the line and the tip of the swing tip should be sunk just below the water level, eliminating any wind drag on the line. Figure 20A shows the first step, which is to cut the two safety pins off to a length of $\frac{3}{4}$″ with the circular hinge portion left on. Choose smallish pins, since the lighter the finished article is, the better and more sensitive it will be.

Bend the pins as at Figure 20B and if preferred, flatten the ends to be whipped on to the rigid section of the tip, with a couple of hammers onè small and one large, the larger hammer being used as an anvil.

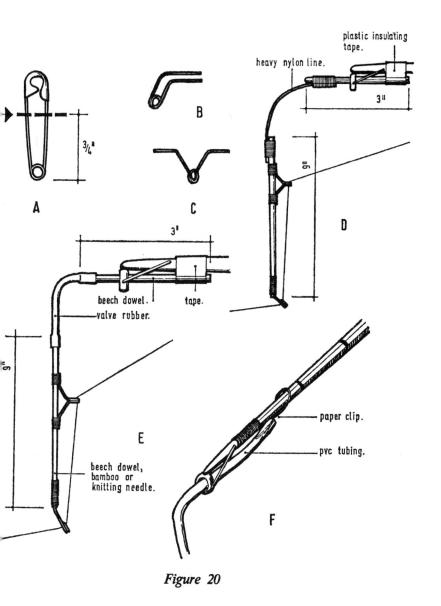

Figure 20

81

Whip the two safety-pin rod rings on to the rigid material, whatever it is you have chosen to use, and paint the rod and whippings with the colour of your fancy.

For fishing late at night or early morning, white or Dayglow yellow show up best, but orange may be a better choice for all-round use. Try white with an orange or red tip, and the addition of a narrow black band helps too.

After painting, varnish and allow to dry thoroughly.

The final operation is to force about ½″ of the rod end into the flexible tubing. P.V.C. tubing softens up well in boiling water and makes it easy to expand the tube larger than its bore size when cold.

If the nylon line has been chosen as the flexible part of the swing tip, this should be whipped to the rigid section before painting. With this type of tip it will be necessary to whip a short length of dowel on to the rod end of the flexible section, giving one a better fixing at the rod tip as illustrated in Figure 20D. Holding and warming near heat or flame will enable a 90° bend to be permanently put into heavy nylon line.

Fixing the swing tip to the rod top can be achieved in two ways:

1. By using a paper clip pushed into the tube end after being expanded over the rod as in Figure 20F.

2. By securing with adhesive plastic tape. The sort sold for electrical insulation is perfect. See Figure 20D and E.

Personally I prefer the second method for all types of swing tips. It is more positive and does not allow the tip to swing about too much.

One final word about this type of tip: it looks neater if the tubing is kept down to a small enough diameter to slip through the tip rod ring.

## SWING TIPS FOR RIVERS

MATERIALS

Approximately 12″ of heavy gauge polythene or alkathene tubing, the type used for waste pipes or water supply. If this is not available, suitable pieces of materials can be cut from an old polythene or alkathene bucket. In fact nearly any soft plastic article (an old toy for example) will yield a suitable piece of material, as long as it is ⅛″ thick or more. Figure 16B shows the approximate size required.

The other materials are similar to those required for the still-water swing tip.

CONSTRUCTION

Prepare the safety pins as before and put them aside.

If plastic tube is being used, proceed as follows:

Put the tube in a vice and, using a fine-toothed saw such as a hacksaw or tenon saw, cut the tube vertically down the middle into two halves.

Now cut a ¼″ wide strip off one edge. This strip will be slightly wedge-shaped in section and the first step is to shape the strip to the sections and taper as in Figure 21B. The shaping is best done using a sharp modelling knife. Finish with coarse and fine sandpaper.

The thicker end is grooved for about 2″ on one side to form a seating on the rod tip. When the plastic is bent to a right-angle, keep this groove on the inside of the bend.

Any flame will provide sufficient heat to soften the plastic for bending, a gas lighter for example, or even a candle. Do not put the plastic into the actual flame, but close enough to soften it for bending. Once bent, a dip in cold water will quickly harden it.

Whip the rings into position, and finish the tip off with either paint, varnish or both.

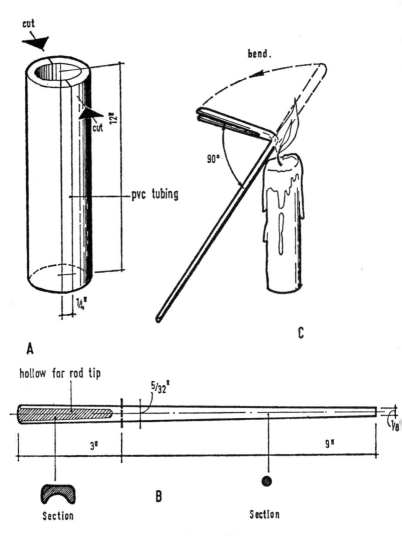

cut

bend.

12"

cut

90°

pvc tubing

¼"

A

C

hollow for rod tip

5/32"

⅛"

3"

9"

Section

B

Section

*Figure 21*

A white or Dayglow colour tip is a great help in dull or failing light.

These swing tips are so easy and quick to make that a whole range of tips of various thicknesses can be produced for the tackle box in a very short time.

## CORK AND BALSA BOBBINS

Although floats and swing tips have their uses and advantages, for really sensitive bite detection, and for convenience, particularly at night, a detector at the reel end of the rod has much to commend it.

The simplest form of detector in this style is the cork bobbin. See Figure 22A.

MATERIALS FOR THE CORK BOBBIN
Any small bottle cork will do.
Approximately 3 ft of light twine.
One metal meat skewer or length of stiff wire to make one.

CONSTRUCTION
Cut the 'V'-shaped slot in the narrow end of the cork with a razor blade or modelling knife. At the bottom of the 'V' cut a slot approximately ¼" deep. Drill a ¼" deep hole, ⅛" diameter in the centre of the wide end. Knot one end of the twine several times in the same spot and dip it in Araldite or similar and force it into the hole in the cork end.

Tie the other end of the twine securely on to the ring of the skewer. Undercoat and paint with either signal yellow or white if to be used for night fishing, and varnish. The detection is then ready for use.

Normally speaking, this type of bobbin is meant to be tied to the front rod rest. I tried this but found that on striking the

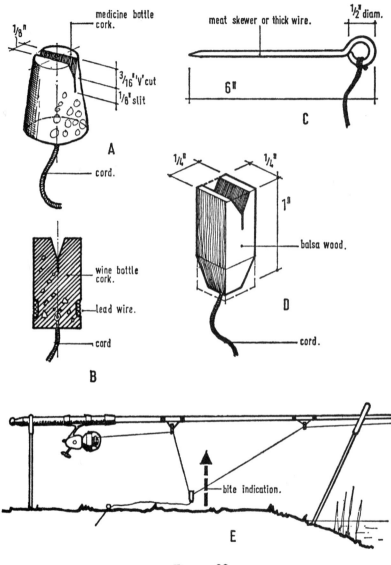

Figure 22

rod, the cork flies off in a forward direction, normally into the water and out of reach without having to get up to retrieve it.

With the skewer fixing, it can be placed well within reach, centrally below the first two rings, this keeps it handy for adjustment and within reach after striking. See Figure 22E.

If you need a heavier bobbin for ledgering into the teeth of a gale, cut a groove around the middle of the cork, wind around with lead wire and paint. See Figure 22B. Personally I have never fished in conditions when a heavy bobbin was necessary, principally because I invariably fish with my rod tip in the water to eliminate line drag completely. The only effect which can give the bobbin false movement is wind on the bobbin itself. I don't feel that a weighted bobbin is the answer: shielding the bobbin from the wind is a better answer, because the heavier the bobbin the more chance there is of the fish feeling the resistance.

A bobbin should be as light as is practicably possible, particularly for night fishing on still-water in conditions of near calm. For this type of fishing I use a small light bobbin made from balsa.

MATERIALS FOR BALSA BOBBIN

$\frac{1}{4}$" square balsa 1" long (or bigger if preferred).
Nylon thread.
Meat skewer as before.

CONSTRUCTION

Construction is exactly similar to the cork bobbin, except that instead of twine, nylon thread is used for the securing line. Finish as before. See Figure 22D.

The smaller the bobbin the better. Assuming conditions are suitable, every tiny movement of the fish nosing the bait will show, particularly in the beam of lantern at night. I have never been convinced yet that fish are attracted by light at night, at least not on lakes; on rivers yes, because lights mean boats and boats mean food scraps. This I feel is the only reason one can give for using a torch to illuminate a float at night.

Even with bobbins, I try to keep my torch light as small as possible and shielded from the water.


## STICK DETECTOR

Perch, bream, carp—all three demand an open baling arm for the best chance of hooking them.

The following bite indicator was suggested in *Angling Times* and its design origin cannot be officially credited to any one person.

I have tried it and it works perfectly but as with other types, is best in calmer conditions, or with the rod tip sunk below water level.


### MATERIALS
12" × ¼" beech dowel.
6" slither of bamboo or hard balsa.
8" 10 lb nylon line.


### CONSTRUCTION
Make a shallow groove ⅜" from one end. Round off the bamboo slither and whip one end of the nylon line to it.

Slightly taper the top of the beech dowel and point the opposite end. Whip the other end of the nylon line to the top of the beech dowel. See Figure 23A and B.

Give the dowel a coat of protective paint and varnish. Colour the bamboo slither white, signal yellow or red, depending on whether it is intended for day or night fishing.

For really sensitive still-water work, replace the bamboo with a 6" length of ⅛" square balsa.

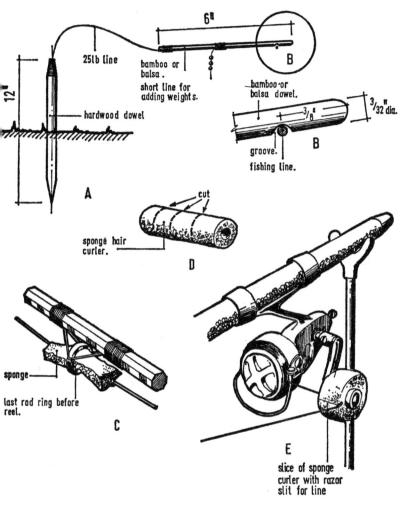

25lb line

6"

B

bamboo or
balsa.

short line for
adding weights.

bamboo or
balsa dowel.

3/32" dia.

3/8"

groove.

fishing line.

B

hardwood dowel

12"

A

cut

sponge hair
curler.

D

sponge

last rod ring before
reel.

C

E

slice of sponge
curler with razor
slit for line

*Figure 23*

89

The rounding of the balsa will prevent any chance of snagging lines. The groove is also necessary to help keep the balsa slipping off the line.

If, when in use, it is found that the angle of the bamboo or balsa is too great, the nylon line may be shortened or a heavier breaking-strain nylon line used.

This is a first-class detector and works well. If you decide to use it in windy weather it will be necessary to make the bamboo slither heavier, either by using a larger diameter piece of bamboo or by whipping an additional length of line as at Figure 23C, and hanging weights on it until the desired results are achieved.

## OPEN REEL LINE CLIP

In recent months angling papers have published letters from anglers who have adapted, designed and used sponge rubber in various forms for ledgering.

One great idea is the use of a piece of sponge rubber as a light bung in the last rod ring. This prevents the effect of wind moving the line through the rings. It should only be pushed into the ring just sufficiently tightly or a biting fish will feel the resistance. See Figure 23C.

Another use of sponge rubber that intrigued me was described by the angler who cut short lengths off a woman's hair curler. This ring was fitted over the reel handle and light razor cuts made around the outside. See Figure 23D and E.

The baling arm is opened after casting and tightening up, the line is taken off the reel and slipped into one of the razor cuts.

The cuts holds the line sufficiently to prevent the breeze moving it, but does not offer resistance to a taking fish.

The only objection I had to using the last idea was the uncanny knack the breeze has of blowing the line into a super-

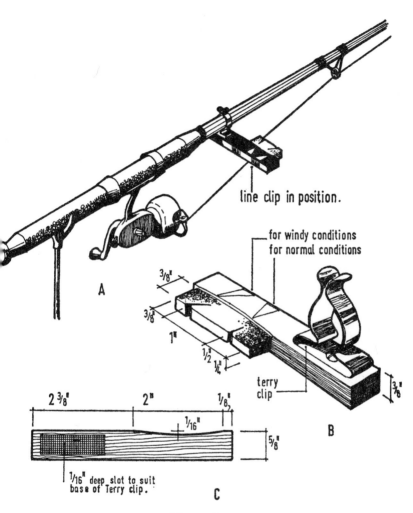

line clip in position.

for windy conditions
for normal conditions

$\frac{3}{8}$"

$\frac{3}{8}$"

1"

$\frac{1}{2}$" $\frac{1}{4}$"

A

terry
clip

$\frac{3}{8}$"

B

$2\frac{3}{8}$"     2"     $\frac{1}{8}$"

$\frac{1}{16}$"

$\frac{5}{8}$"

$\frac{1}{16}$" deep slot to suit
base of Terry clip.

C

*Figure 24*

91

tangle with baling arm hinge, or some other projection on the reel.

This set me thinking that there must be a simpler way to use sponge rubber as a line clip, and to keep the line away from the reel. The following gadget works, and is of particular use in windy weather.

MATERIALS

MATERIALS
One Terry clip to fit rod 3" in front of reel.
$3'' \times \frac{5}{8}'' \times \frac{3}{8}''$ hardwood.
$1\frac{1}{2}'' \times \frac{3}{8}'' \times \frac{1}{4}''$ plastic sponge.

CONSTRUCTION
Smooth up the square timber section and round off all sharp corners. Figure 24c shows a $\frac{1}{10}''$ shallow dishing that has to be $\frac{1}{8}''$ in from one end on one side only. When the plastic sponge is stuck into this dishing it gives just the right amount of grip to the line.

Screw the Terry clip into place; if additional insurance against the clip moving is required, sit the base of the clip into a $\frac{1}{16}''$ deep groove chiselled into the top of the square timber section.

Using impact adhesive, stick the plastic sponge into position. With a razor blade make two cuts in positions shown half the depth of the sponge—one cut at right-angles to the timber, and the outside cut at an angle of 60°. See Figure 24B.

The prototype was painted matt black with white arrows pointing towards the cuts. These arrows can be painted in any light signal colour.

The straight slot nearest the rod is for normal use in average conditions and the outer angled slot for windy weather.

Method of use is to hold the line, open the baling arm on

the reel, lift the line up and slip it into the slot in the sponge. See Figure 24A.

The straight slot offers just enough resistance to prevent breeze and line drag moving the line from the slot, but a taking fish will do so.

This is particularly useful for perch or eel fishing with a ledger.

# CHAPTER FIVE

# Simple electric detectors

This chapter is devoted to the simplest forms of electric bite detectors.

Every angler, keen enough to fish at night, has his own preference for the type of detection he uses. Some of the largest coarse fish caught, worthy of a mention in 'how I did it' books and fishing magazines, were caught using a piece of silver paper folded over the line as a detector.

However, we are in the age of flights to the moon and computers, and it is logical to try and introduce a little modern thinking into bite detection.

For some years now, there have been a number of types of electrical detectors available in tackle shops. Most of them are very expensive for the average angler who likes an occasional spot of night fishing. Not only are they expensive, but some are very bulky and heavy to carry about. With a little ingenuity, home-built detectors can be made that are neither expensive nor bulky.

Construction is easy, once the basic method of connecting a bulb or a buzzer to a battery has been mastered.

## ILLUMINATED BOBBIN

The finished weight of a bobbin is the factor that determines what kind of fishing it can be used for. Naturally, for any fish other than pike, perch and eels, it should be as light as possible.

Two types of bobbin will now be described, with some suggestions for further experiment.

MATERIALS

A small plastic box with sliding or removable lid, or a small plastic tube with a stopper. These can be containers of anything from small replacement parts for drawing pens, to pill bottles.

A *small* torch bulb, whose voltage is the same as the battery to be used, and as low a wattage as possible (Christmas tree lights replacement bulbs are useful).

Or if a really small bobbin is to be made, a miniature Edisan screw, a doll's-house bulb and holder, obtainable from any good hobby model shop, or do-it-yourself store.

About 1' 6" of fine flexible screened wire, similar to that used for transistor radio or deaf-aid earphone pieces. Any radio spares department can supply this.

A battery to match voltage of bulb.

CONSTRUCTION

The first step is to ensure that when the bulb is in its socket, there is going to be sufficient room in the plastic box. Remember that a soldered connection has to be made to the bottom of the holder, and if all is well, it is a good idea to make a single knot close up under the holder to keep the soldered connection from getting broken.

95

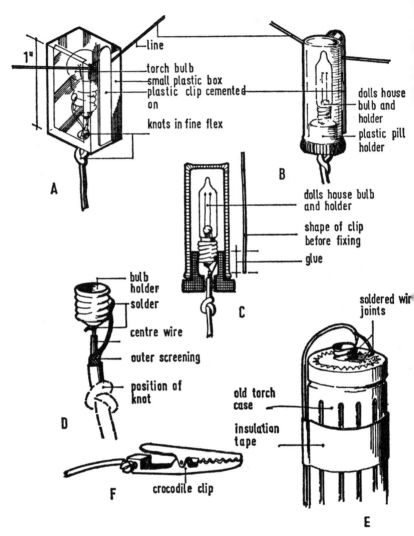

line
torch bulb
small plastic box
plastic clip cemented on
knots in fine flex

dolls house bulb and holder
plastic pill holder

A

B

dolls house bulb and holder
shape of clip before fixing
glue

C

bulb holder
solder
centre wire
outer screening
position of knot

soldered wire joints

old torch case
insulation tape

D

F          crocodile clip

E

*Figure 25*

Drill a hole, large enough to accept the flex, in the bottom of the bobbin case, and start to prepare the bobbin end of the flex for soldering.

By carefully cutting down to the outer screening flex through the plastic outer sleeving, bare approximately $\frac{1}{2}''$ of wire.

Starting at the top, use a pin to unpick the braid of the sleeving and wind $\frac{1}{4}''$ of it together to one side of the wire.

This operation exposes the inner plastic insulation, and $\frac{1}{8}''$ of this should be carefully removed leaving the inner wire clear for soldering.

Using the technique described in the first chapter, solder the leads to the holder as shown in Figure 25D.

Now tie a single knot as close under the holder as you can and thread the battery end of the wire through the hole in the bottom of the bobbin. A second single knot tight up against the underside of the bobbin secures the bulb permanently in place.

The battery end of the flex can be organised in a number of different ways, depending on what you have available for holding a battery. It should preferably be something with a switch. Figure 25E shows the way the prototype was soldered to a small torch which takes a No. 8 battery.

The top part of the torch was removed, and this contained the glass and reflector. No bulb was required and the centre wire was soldered to the bulb holder and the outer screen to the case of the torch. The flex was then taped to the side of the torch to prevent the connections from being torn away in use.

For use at night, particularly if it is damp, seal the torch in a plastic bag with a rubber band.

Other types of torches can be used, a bicycle lamp for instance or an old rear lamp. Alternatively, purchase two crocodile clips as shown in Figure 25F, and connect two short lengths of ordinary lamp flex to them, and the other ends to the bared ends of the bobbin flex by twisting or soldering. A short piece of tape round each joint and a longer piece to hold both together, protect it from dampness.

Crocodile clips can be used on any battery which has brass strips as contacts.

Finally, the bobbin needs a clip to enable you to attach it to the fishing line. This is achieved using a suitable length of stiffish plastic slightly longer than the length of the bobbin and glued to the bobbin, at the bottom only, with Araldite.

If the plastic has a slight curve towards the bobbin before glueing (see Figure 25c), it is held in place with a clothes peg while the glue sets. A good grip on the fishing line is then assured.

## SIMPLE DETECTOR HEAD

The most important part of any electric bite detector is the head unit. Many angling books refer to this type of detector and some have a brief description. None, as far as I know, give clear enough details to enable the average angler to make one.

The detector head which is the subject of this section, has been in use, quite successfully, by the author, for several years now. It serves as the switch for any of the visual or audible signals described later. It is particularly suitable for carp fishing, or for any species that takes the bait and runs, stops, and then runs again (perch or eels for example). When the fish runs the signal comes on, when the fish stops the detector head switches off and the signal ceases, coming on again when the fish next runs.

The detector head described here has been reduced down to its most simple form; this is based on the principle that the simpler it is, the less there is to go wrong.

At the end of this section are some suggestions for making

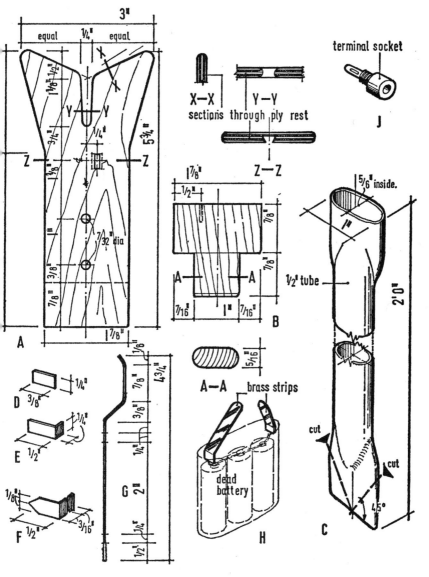

*Figure 26*

99

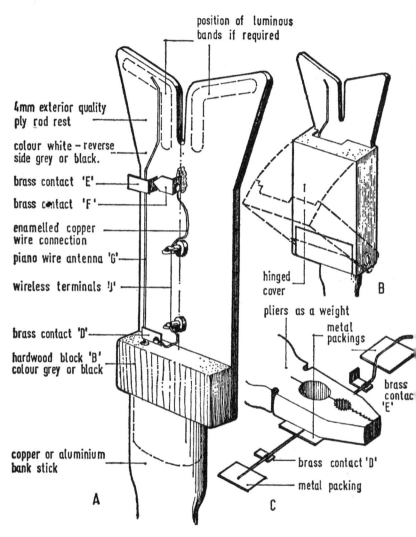

Figure 27

100

the head a little more sophisticated but whether you carry them out or not is up to you.

MATERIALS

6" × 3" of 4 mm ply (marine ply is more resistant to dampness and should be used if available).
2" × 2" of ½" hardwood—mahogany for example or obeche.
5" of 32 gauge piano wire.
2 small pieces of 30 gauge flat brass ¼" wide (flat battery contact strips are perfect).
2 radio sockets (radio spares).
2 short lengths of copper connecting wires—plastic covered.
Approximately 2' length of aluminium tube ½" bore (copper pipe may be used but is heavier to carry).

CONSTRUCTION

Transfer the full size shape of the detector head (shown in Figure 26A) on to the ply.

This can be done by drawing out the shape on tracing paper and transferring it to the ply with carbon paper.

Cut the shape out with a fret saw or coping saw, and round off the edges of the shape to the sections shown, with a rasp or glasspaper.

The second step is to form the base section from the hardwood. Mark out the shape on one side and cut out as before. The smaller bottom section has now to be shaped to the section shown, so that it will fit snugly into the flattened top of the aluminium tube bank stick.

Make the bank stick before shaping the hardwood.

Flattening should be done using a hammer and tapping the tube on a hard surface. Tap both sides of the tube to get an even shape and measure it occasionally to ensure a final width across the narrow part of $\frac{5}{16}$".

101

The bottom of the bank stick is completely flattened and the corners cut off with a hacksaw to an angle of 45°. Clean up with a fine file and the job is complete.

The hardwood end can now be tailored, using a chisel and glasspaper, to a perfect hand-tight fit.

Glue the hardwood block to the bottom of the ply using Araldite, and set it aside to dry in a warm place (a radiator or boiler top). While you are waiting, the pieces of brass strip and the antenna can be prepared. One source of brass strip are the contacts from the top of a dead flat battery: they can be pulled off with a pair of pliers.

Cut, bend and file the brass into the three shapes shown, smoothing off any rough edges with a fine file or emery cloth.

Cut a 5″ length of the piano wire, and bend it to the shape in Figure 26G, make sure the wire is straight and not curved or bent when viewed from the side.

Take the two radio spares sockets and remove the nuts; these are not required.

Assuming that sufficient time has elapsed for the adhesive to set, take the timber part and drill the small hole for the antenna. The initial hole may have to be made at a slight angle, unless you have made it before glueing the timber sections together. The hole can be straightened up by tapping in a longish panel pin a bit at a time and wobbling it round the hole.

Having satisfied yourself that the hole is deep enough for the wire, leaving clearance below the lower brass strip, cut the small slot $\frac{1}{4}″ \times \frac{1}{16}″ \times \frac{1}{8}″$ deep to receive the pointed brass contact.

Set the wire and brass strips up on metal packs as shown in Figure 27C. It is essential to 'tin' the parts of brass strip and the wire as described in Chapter 1. The soldering will then be a very simple matter.

Use a pair of pliers or similar tool to hold the wire down, and solder the brass strips in position, keeping them in the same place as the bends in the wire.

When the solder is cold, which will be almost immediately, clean off as much of the flux as possible with petrol, for example, on a piece of wadding; this will prevent the corrosive action of the flux from starting.

Mix up a small amount of Plastic Padding and fill the hole for the wire and the slot for the brass contact, use a piece of wire or a pointed match-stick to force the adhesive in. Push the wire and the brass contact into place, and pack if necessary to keep in position until the Plastic Padding has set, which will be in a few minutes. Glue the radio spares sockets into place as shown in Figure 27A.

Finishing the item is a matter of personal preference. The prototype was primed and then painted white on the bank face, and grey elsewhere.

To use the detector head, position it on its bank stick so that one of the larger rod rings can be placed very close behind the antenna. See Figure 29A on page 108. When a fish takes the bait and moves off with it, the line tends to straighten; this action pulls the antenna across and completes the circuit, setting off the alarm signal, either light or buzzer. The gap between the brass contacts can be adjusted by bending either the antenna or the pointed brass contact. It is possible to adjust the sensitivity so that the signal can be activated even with the baling arm off.

Two refinements that can be carried out are:

1. Luminous painted strips are added to the front faces of the rod rest. This was used on the prototype. It is useful on a very dark night but the luminosity does tend to fade very quickly. See Figure 27A.

2. A very useful refinement is a swing-down cover, hinged with two small brass round-head screws. This can be made from $\frac{1}{16}''$ plywood glued together with Plastic Padding fillets on the inside. An alternative is to make the width and height of the detector head suit an empty metal cover which held, say, pencils. Clear plastic boxes have been tried but they tend to be very brittle and break easily. Paint finish the ply or

metal case as before. Don't forget to cut the slot for the antenna large enough for it to move freely without touching the case. See Figure 27B for a general view.

## LIGHT SIGNAL UNIT

For those anglers who wish to use a bite detector at night only, and do not intend to leave the vicinity of their rod, the light signal is quite adequate. It does have one disadvantage over a buzzer unit—there is the possibility of alarming the fish with a flashing light. Some anglers will feel this reason important enough to prefer the buzzer unit to be described in section marked 'Buzzer Signal'.

MATERIALS

A rectangular 2 oz tobacco tin.

$\frac{7}{8}'' \times 13\frac{1}{2}''$ of stiff cardboard or fibreboard approximately $\frac{1}{16}''$ thick.

$\frac{7}{8}'' \times 2''$ of stiff cardboard.

One bulb holder (Woolworths).

2 small pieces of brass strip approximately $\frac{3}{8}'' \times \frac{1}{4}''$.

2 terminal sockets (radio spares).

2 short lengths of plastic-covered copper connecting wire.

1 flat flashlamp battery and bulb to suit.

1 plastic hemisphere (part of a child's toy or rear lamp).

CONSTRUCTION

Form the cardboard strip to fit the curves inside the box, making the joint in the centre of one short side.

Cut two $\frac{1}{4}''$ square holes in the card at the corners to accept the battery more snugly.

Glue the cardboard into place using Evo-stick. When dry, drill the two holes, through tin and card, to accept the ter-

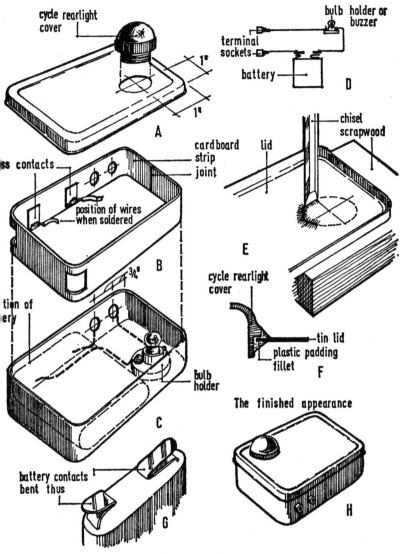

*Figure 28*

minal plugs and fix them into place with the nuts provided. Using Evo-stick, glue the brass contacts into place as shown in Figure 28B, in such a position that the bent brass contacts on the battery make a good contact with the brass strips.

Mix a small quantity of Araldite and glue the bulb holder down on the bottom of the box, centrally, below where the hole in the lid will be.

The next step is to wire the bulb holder and sockets to each of the brass strips as shown in Figure 28c. The wires should be kept into the corners of the tin and follow the paths shown by the dotted lines in the sketch.

Finally, cut the hole in the lid for the coloured plastic signal. The size will depend on the shape of the plastic dome you have found to use.

Cut out the hole with a small chisel and mallet, working round a scribed hole on the inside of the lid. See Figure 28E.

Before cutting, put a piece of scrap softwood under the hole position.

The edges of the hole can be enlarged and cleaned up with a fine circular file (rat's tail file).

Secure the plastic dome to the lid using Plastic Padding; a small fillet of the material both inside and out will ensure a permanent fixture.

Paint the tin any chosen colour, undercoat first and gloss to finish. Of course there is no need to paint the tin at all but doing so does make it look less like a tobacco tin and helps to protect it from moisture.

The box you use to contain either the light or the buzzer unit does not need to be a tobacco tin. Any suitable container will do; a plastic sandwich box, a cigar box, or even a fairly strong card box will do. Naturally the latter will suffer if it is allowed to get damp, but in inclement weather it should be protected with a plastic bag.

One final tip: in order to ensure good electrical contact between battery and brass strips, some folded cardboard packing may be necessary between the bottom of the battery and side of the tin box.

## CONNECTING THE UNITS

Normally speaking 1½ yards of twin flex will be ample for the connection. Later in this chapter the use of units at long range will be described, when longer leads are required.

MATERIALS

1½ yards of twin plastic covered lighting flex.
4 wireless plugs, to suit sockets in units (radio spares).

CONSTRUCTION

Cut carefully around plastic insulation and strip off about ¾″ of it to expose the wire. Twist the wire with the fingers in the direction it is wound to tighten it up.

Unscrew the plastic plug top, and slide it up the flex. Figure 29c. Pass the wire through the loop in the metal plug part '2' and twist the flex tightly as '4'. Slide '3' up over '2' and screw '1' down tightly on to '3'.

Treat all four ends of the flex similarly and the connection lead is ready.

Plug the two units together as in Figure 29A, cast out, open the baling arm and set line over the antenna as previously described. Test by giving the line in front of the buzzer head a pull. Now wait for that first run—it could be the biggest carp you have ever seen!

107

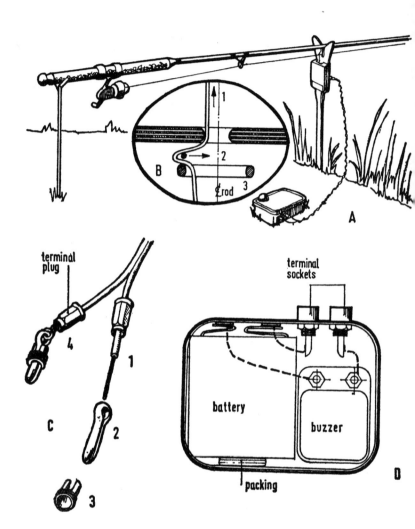

*Figure 29*

## BUZZER SIGNAL

Basically, materials and construction are exactly similar to the light signal unit, except that a buzzer replaces the bulb holder. This unit may be preferred by the angler who considers that the minimum disturbance is essential, particularly the specimen hunter, after carp for example.

### MATERIALS

These are as for the light unit, but replace the bulb holder with a small 4½-volt buzzer. The buzzer in the prototype was an ex-W.D. unit from a radio shop dealing in this type of goods.

Most radio shops that sell spares for amateur constructors will have a buzzer unit in stock. The size of one type of buzzer unit which is readily available is 1⅜″ × 1¼″ × ¾″ thick and is made in England.

### CONSTRUCTION

Follow the instruction for the light unit, with the exception of the hole in the lid and the plastic signal. Naturally, the buzzer unit is glued down in place of the bulb holder, but is wired up in the same way. See Figure 29D.

It is a good idea to check the buzzer immediately after purchase by wiring it to the battery. If it does not work, it saves a great deal of fruitless effort to discover it is faulty before completion.

## THREE-ROD JUNCTION BOX

If one is night fishing, particularly if specimen hunting, more than one rod is certain to be used.

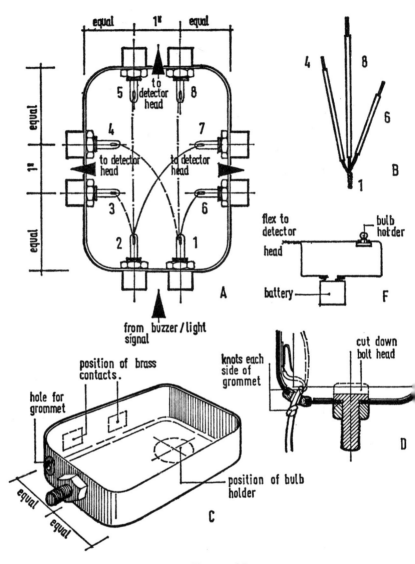

*Figure 30*

Eel fishing with two or three rods is another example when the junction box will come in useful.

Some anglers will insist on having a separate buzzer or light signal for each rod, but there are those who, from the weight consideration alone, would be quite happy with one buzzer or light unit to serve two or three detector heads.

The one disadvantage of this is that it is necessary, as soon as the signal is seen, to inspect each rod in turn to determine which one the bite is on. A piece of silver paper on the line of each rod, just lying on the ground below the reel will give an instant indication, visible even at night, of which rod the fish is on. Just look for the piece of silver paper that is either moving, or has gone.

MATERIALS
One rectangular 2 oz tobacco tin.
8 terminal sockets (radio spares—2 red and 6 black).
2′ of plastic-covered single flex.

CONSTRUCTION
This unit is very simple to construct; the hard work is merely the drilling of eight holes to accept the threaded portion of the sockets. Secure all eight sockets in place with the nuts provided. See Figure 30A.

Take the plastic-covered connecting wire and cut off two lengths slightly longer than required to run from sockets 1–6, 1–8 and 1–4 and separate into two groups of three different lengths. Strip about ½″ of plastic covering from each end of all six wires, still keeping them in separate groups. Figure 30B.

Twist one end of the three wires in each group together and solder the twisted ends to socket 1 and the other to socket 2.

Now solder each wire to its respective terminal and remove

111

as much flux as possible as described for the detector head.

If you have used the red sockets for Nos. 1 and 2 this is all you need to identify the correct ones to wire up to the light or buzzer unit.

Test the unit by connecting up the light or buzzer unit, and a single wire with terminal plugs at each end across each pair of sockets in turn. Alternatively use a twin connecting lead and just touch the two end plugs together.

Finish the unit as before. A bright colour is preferable, so that it shows up at night. This will prevent a nasty accident during an evening's fishing.

For the same reason, it is a good idea to use white plastic-covered flex for connecting up the units. It is uncanny the way the flex seems to wind itself around your feet at night; therefore the more clearly it shows up, the easier it is to step across, and avoid an unexpected midnight swim.

## LONG RANGE LIGHT SIGNAL

There are times, e.g., specimen hunting, when a second rod is used some distance away from the swim at which you have made camp. Since a buzzer would be useless, unless it is loud enough to wake the dead, a light signal is the obvious choice.

The type of mounting you use depends on the height the signal needs to be above ground to be visible from camp. You can fix a loop of wire to it and hang it from a convenient branch.

However the unit to be described was made for the lake I fish regularly, and a screw fitting was used to suit a standard bank stick.

Another variation with this unit is that the sockets have been omitted and the flex is connected direct to the unit. However, you could retain the sockets if you wish.

MATERIALS

Use the same materials as for the light signal unit but omit the two terminal sockets and add :

2 terminal plugs (radio spares).

3 yards of thin plastic covered flex.

1 small rubber grommet.

1 bolt with $\frac{3}{8}''$ diameter thread to suit a standard bank stick.

1 nut to suit the last item.


CONSTRUCTION

Build the battery contacts exactly as before, but instead of drilling two holes for terminal sockets, drill only one hole of a size to accept the rubber grommet. Drill a second hole large enough to accept the bolt at the bottom of the unit, and in the centre both ways. See Figure 30 c and d.

Unless the bolt has a thin head this may need to be cut down to about $\frac{1}{8}''$ thickness. Do this with a hacksaw, holding the nut in a vice. With care and patience this can be done fairly easily, and it will need to be smoothed off with a fine file to take off the rough edges. See Figure 30d.

If the head of the bolt is left at its full thickness, there will not be enough room in the box for the other fittings. Complete the construction of the unit, and bare the four ends of flex ready for connection.

One wire is soldered to one side of the bulb holder and the other to the battery contact, replacing the terminal socket connections in the earlier unit.

Make a single knot in the flex close to the connections, but far enough away to leave some slack wire within the box, when the knot is close against the grommet inside it.

Pass the wire through the grommet from the inside of the box, and make a second knot close against the outside of the grommet.

113

This will ensure that the flex connections cannot be pulled apart in use. See Figure 30D.

Finally fit the two plugs to the other end of the flex and the unit is ready for painting.

# CHAPTER SIX

# More advanced electric detectors

The items that follow are the most complicated in this book. This does not mean that they are beyond the ability of the reader, but it is suggested that some of the simpler electrical items should be made first.

Once the knack of wiring-up, making soldered joints and generally getting the earlier units to work has been mastered, the more complex units will be relatively easy.

## MERCURY FLIP SWITCH

Once eels and perch have taken the bait they rarely fail to be caught. They make two or more runs after which the angler strikes and the fight begins.

The detector head, previously described, is primarily intended as a tool for the specimen hunter or night angler fishing for carp or tench. This unit is a more definite, and in some ways simpler, piece of equipment. Once the fish has taken even a short run the buzzer will go or the light signal will stay on until the angler switches it off.

This makes it a most suitable companion for the long range light signal, for with the normal detector head you might

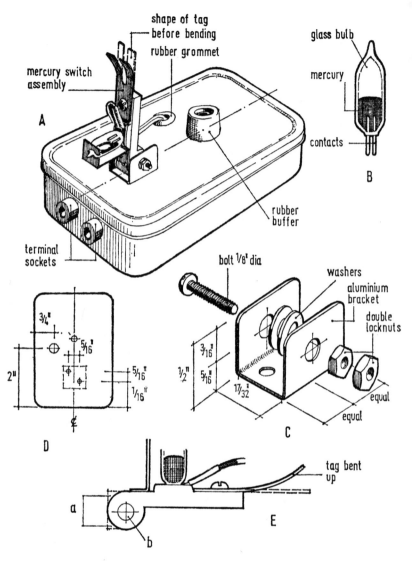

*Figure 31*

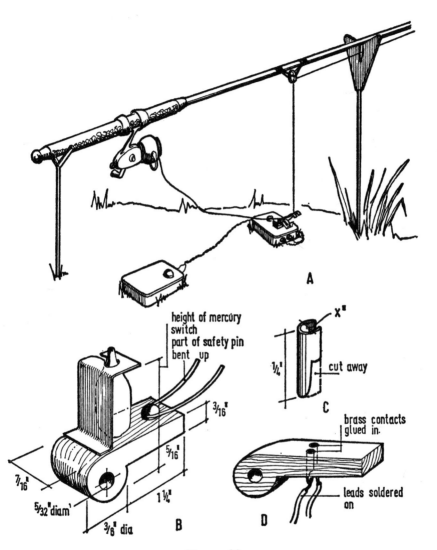

*Figure 32*

117

miss the first brief flash of the signal, the fish might lie doggo and you would be unaware you had had a bite.

Not so with the flip switch; it switches on at the first run and doesn't stop until you turn it off.

The basic main part of a mercury switch is a small glass tube with two separate electrical contacts at one end passing through the glass to the outside, in a similar fashion to a bulb. Also inside the tube is a small globule of mercury.

Depending on the position the tube is in, the mercury can be away from the contacts, in which case no current will flow or covering both of them and making a circuit.

### MATERIALS

The unit is built around a mercury switch which is to be found as part of a number of makes of door chimes. It may be purchased as a spare part from most electrical dealers. Another source of supply is the ex-W.D. shop, and although it may not be part of a hinged unit as the door chime accessory, a little imagination will quickly find a way of using it.

One mercury switch is required per unit.

2 6" lengths of soft flexible connecting wire: cotton/silk or rubber covered.

1 rubber button (a lavatory seat buffer will do).

2 terminal sockets (radio spares).

3 small nuts and bolts.

1 rectangular 2 oz tobacco tin.

$\frac{1}{32}$" sheet aluminium $\frac{5}{8}$" × $1\frac{5}{8}$" for 'U' bracket.

### CONSTRUCTION

The construction of this unit depends on the type of mercury switch you are able to acquire.

For the purpose of this section it will be assumed that a suitable switch from an old door chime has been found

It will look similar to Figure 31A, and requires very little work to prepare it for the switch.

All that needs to be done is to file off the corners of the plastic at 'a', obtain a bolt which is an easy sliding fit in the hole at 'b', or the hole can be carefully drilled out to receive a bolt. Finally a curve should be imparted to the pronged brass strip at 'E'.

Next prepare the aluminium 'U' bracket. This is best bent up in a vice, around a piece of wood, the thickness of which should give adequate clearance to the plastic of the mercury switch.

After you are satisfied that the switch will be a loose fit in the bracket, drill the holes for the swivel bolt and the fixings.

The bolts which are to be used for fixing the bracket down, may need their heads reduced in height. This can be done fairly easily with a fine file. An alternative is to reduce the amount of plastic at the bottom of the mercury switch when it is in the vertical position, so that it will swing freely without jamming.

Place the bracket in position on the lid of the tobacco tin, and mark the position of *one* hole. Drill this hole and bolt the bracket in place. The second hole can now be drilled through the bracket and the final bolt fitted.

Drill the lid for the rubber grommet and fit this.

The final touch is to glue the rubber buffer into position and bolt the mercury switch into place. If you leave sufficient space to fit a small washer on either side of the switch there is a better chance of a smooth action. Use two nuts on the end of the bolt, and tighten one against the other—this will prevent the single nut from working loose, and allow you to leave plenty of clearance between nut and bracket.

The last job is to drill the holes for the terminal sockets and fit them as on previous units.

Wire the twin-flexible leads through the grommet and solder to the terminals. If the existing leads on the switch are short they can be extended with a short length of ordinary twin flex.

To use, make a cast and tighten up. The switch should be lifted vertically and the unit placed about 2' away and to one side of the rod between the reel and the first ring. Open the baling arm and draw off sufficient line to hook between the prongs. The first bite will pull the line and flip the switch down and set off the signal—the rest is up to you! See Figure 32A.

Figure 31B shows an enlarged drawing of the mercury switch proper. Assuming the door chime part is not obtainable, only the switch and holder, a little ingenuity must be exercised. Try making a piece of hardwood shaped like the plastic part of the switch and fitted to a similar bracket. A safety pin cut and bent as Figure 32B makes a simple prong —this can be bolted to the thin end of the hardwood.

The contacts for the base of the mercury switch are a little more difficult to make, and I can only suggest a way it might be done, since I have not made an actual switch unit myself.

Try bending up two small pieces of brass from old flat battery contacts as shown in Figure 32C.

Make the diameter at 'x' just large enough to accept the contacts as a tight fit, and glue them into two small holes spaced the same distance apart as the contacts.

Make sure the tag is long enough to project just below the wood, to enable the soldered joint to be made.

Lastly, make the switch holder from thin aluminium or tinplate, the slot at the side being just large enough to let the top thin end of the glass envelope slide in. This can be glued down on to the wood with Araldite as shown in Figure 32B.

Once the unit is assembled a test will show if everything works smoothly. If not, ease any tight spots by re-drilling or sandpapering.

A coat of varnish on the hardwood will prevent dampness from swelling it. Paint the tin as previously described.

## COMBINED LIGHT AND BUZZER UNIT

In order to cater for the angler who wishes to have the choice of light or buzzer signal, this unit combines both, with the possibility of switching from one to the other. The switch can be omitted, of course, which only means a light and a buzz simultaneously when a fish bites. This can be a decided advantage, especially at night, and if the angler takes the precaution of screening the unit from the water, the light will not alarm the fish.

The materials required are those for the buzzer unit previously described, with the addition of the following:

MATERIALS
1 bulb holder and 4½-volt bulb.
1 miniature two-way switch (radio and T.V. spares shop).
1 short length of extra flex.

CONSTRUCTION
As a first step, drill and file the holes in the tin for the terminal sockets and two-way switch. Temporarily place the major parts in the box to determine the final position for the bulb holder. Mark this position on the lid, and cut the hole to accept the domed plastic cover.

Cut the stiff card for the liner strip, try it in position and mark the position of the holes in the tin. Cut these out with a trimming knife and smooth off any hairy edges with fine sandpaper.

Line the inside edge of the tin with the card as before. See Figure 33B. Glue on the brass contacts but in a different position than before. Figure 33A shows the new position. This means that the battery is turned around, making a very neat fit against a buzzer which is no more than 1⅜″ maximum

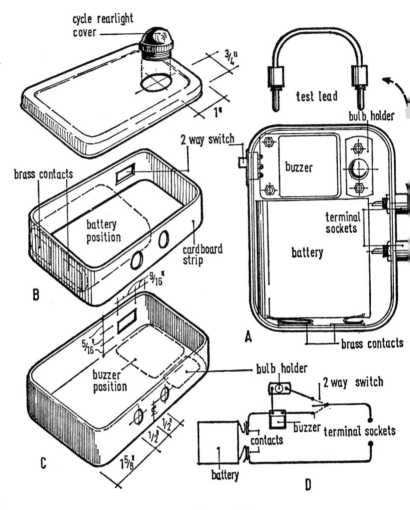

*Figure 33*

width. If the buzzer to be used is wider than this, a larger tin will have to be used. This may then require a little ingenuity on the part of the reader to pack the new size box out with pieces of suitably-sized balsa wood, to get the battery to make a good contact.

Assuming a 2 oz tobacco tin is being used, and a suitable buzzer has been purchased, proceed to solder the two leads from the brass contacts, one long enough to reach the nearest plug socket and the second to reach one terminal on the buzzer.

With Araldite, glue the two-way switch into place and when set solder a lead from the centre contacts to the second terminal socket.

Prepare two short leads, both with loops at one end and straight tinned ends at the other, for connecting to the switch.

From one side of the switch, one lead goes to the second buzzer terminal and the other to one bulb holder terminal.

Remember when wiring-up, to keep the wires as close a fit as possible into the corners of the tin, except when there is space above the units.

Connect these last two leads just prior to fixing the buzzer and bulb holder in position with Araldite. Put it aside to set.

Take the lid and fix the domed bulb cover in with Plastic Padding as previously described.

Only one electrical connection remains to be fitted: this is the one between the second terminal on the bulb holder and the first terminal on the buzzer.

Fit the bulb, bend the brass contacts on the battery, and place it in position. The unit is now ready for testing and it is suggested that a test lead be made up as 33A, using a piece of single flex with a plug at each end.

The test lead will short-out the terminal sockets, and by moving the switch across, the reader can readily see if it is working correctly. In one position the light should come on, and in the second the buzzer should sound. If something is wrong, check *each* connection and the circuit. To help you do this, and to assist in the initial wiring-up, a theoretical wiring diagram is shown in 33D.

In order to gain the maximum amount of space adjacent to the buzzer, it is necessary to cut off at least one, and probably two sides, off the bulb holder. Assuming it is a plastic one, this can be achieved with a fine hacksaw.

Undercoat, and finish the unit in the colour of your choice and you have a combination with the head unit described earlier, equal to proprietary models costing £2.25 or more— and just as temperamental!

If the reader prefers to have both light and buzzer to come on together, the two-way switch can be omitted. In some ways this is more convenient and it does make construction simpler.

## ROD REST DETECTOR

It always seemed to me so unnecessary to have two separate units making up bite detectors: the head unit and the signal unit joined by a wire.

There are two units to carry, plus the connecting wire which seems always cursed to lose a plug at the most crucial time— in the dark, just as you go to plug in.

**MATERIALS**
All those as mentioned in *The Combined Light and Buzzer Unit* except the two radio sockets, which are not required.
$\frac{1}{4}$" plywood $7\frac{1}{4}$" × $3\frac{1}{8}$".
Plastic, push button, on/off switch (Woolworths).
$\frac{3}{16}$" plywood 1" × $\frac{3}{4}$".
$\frac{3}{8}$" × $\frac{1}{4}$" hardwood 1" long.
30 swg piano wire 6" long (see *Detector Head Unit*) on p. 99.
Small pieces of brass strip (see *Detector Head Unit*) on p. 99.

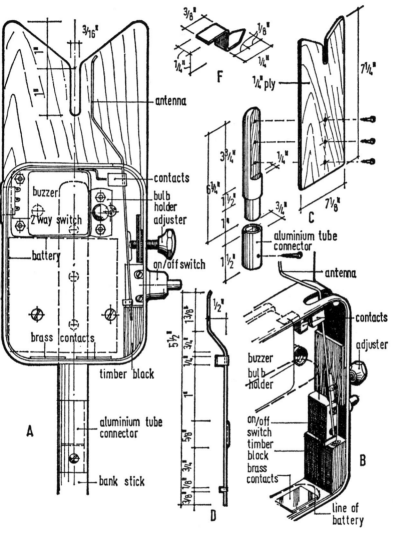

*Figure 34*

125

⅛th Whitworth or similar set screw ⅝″ long.

One small plastic toothpaste or similar tube cap.

Extra plastic-covered connection wire and some short pieces of enamel-covered connecting wire.

2″ of aluminium tube the same diameter as a 3′ length of ¾″ diameter beech dowel rod.

One r/h brass screw.

CONSTRUCTION

Although the construction follows that of the previous unit pretty closely, there are some extra holes to cut and one major initial job to do: that of making and fitting the rod rest section to the tin box.

Mark out the shape of the rod rest on the ply and cut out with a fretsaw or coping saw. Round off all the corners coming into contact with the rod or line and smooth down with sandpaper. Cut all the holes in the tin for the fitting as before, including the new holes for on/off switch and antenna wire etc., and glue and fit the card lining with holes to match as before.

Study Figure 34A and you will see that the card lining in this unit has been omitted three-quarters of the length of the side with the antenna on. The lower end is held down by the shaped hardwood block and the upper end is held back by the small ply rectangle.

Drill or punch four small holes in the base of the tin box in the positions shown, and screw the tin to the ply with the shortest No. 8 woodscrews you can obtain. If the points of the screws show through the other side, file them down flat to the wood. Use countersunk screws as there is not enough room in the box for raised or round-head screws. Trim the ply neatly to the shape of the tin box on the bottom and sides and smooth off. Unscrew the tin and set the screws aside in a safe place.

Now you have to make a decision about the bank stick—

whether to have it attached to the detector permanently, or whether to make the detector detachable.

We will assume you wish to make the latter, which does make the unit a little more portable, although even kept in one piece the unit will slip into the rod bag quite easily, as long as you don't carry too many rods with you.

Cut off 6" from the beech dowel and saw out the ¼" deep rebate. Round off and smooth the top. Next, saw a shallow cut all around the bottom of the dowel and reduce it down with chisel or rasp, so that when smooth it will be a reasonably tight fit in the aluminium tube. This is the removable part of the unit so don't make it too tight a fit, but tight enough to prevent it being loose in use.

When you are satisfied about the fit, glue and pin the ply to the dowel and set aside to set. Make sure the dowel is in a perfectly central position on the centre line of the ply.

Take the remaining piece of dowel, point one end and reduce the other ⅞" long, to be a tight fit in the aluminium tube. Drill a small hole in the tube to take a ¾" round-headed brass screw. Glue and screw this in place and the bank stick part is complete.

Rather than try to put all the fittings into the box with the ply attached to it, try to do as much as possible before you need to fit the buzzer or bulb holder.

Start by shaping the hardwood block to be a neat fit into the curve of the tin and rebate the bottom over the lower edge of the card lining.

Drill a small ⅜" deep hole to accept the antenna, bearing in mind that when the antenna is in position, it has to be clear of the on/off switch. See Figure 34A and B.

Don't glue the block in place yet, until all the other equipment is in place. Fit the on/off switch, keeping it as close against the back as possible. Rebate the narrow edge of the small ply block so that it fits neatly over the top of the tin, glue it into position with Araldite and leave it to set. A small 'G' clamp will hold this exactly where you want it. Now is the time to solder the brass contacts and tags on to the antenna. Figure 34D shows the position of them. The method is the same as that described in the detector head section with the addition of the curved plate that accepts the end of the adjusting screw.

Glue the antenna into position in the hardwood block with Araldite or Plastic Padding and glue the assembly into the tin with Araldite. Make sure the bend in the antenna is parallel with the front face of the tin, and the brass contact is square with the inside of the tin. Use a small 'G' clamp to hold the block in place while it sets.

Make the adjusting screw next, using the set screw and the toothpaste tube cap. Remove the cork sealing disc from inside the cap and glue it on to the head of the screw with Araldite and set it aside to set.

Drill a hole through the ply, using the hole in the tin as a guide, slightly smaller in diameter than the adjusting screw. When the screw is screwed carefully and squarely through the hole, it should strike the centre of the curved plate on the antenna.

Make the pointed brass strip from an old flat battery contact, bend it to the Z shape shown in Figure 34F and glue into place to give about $\frac{1}{16}''$ clearance from the antenna contact when the adjusting screw is completely undone.

Check that the bend of the contact is just clear of the buzzer when it is placed in position, and at the same time, check that when the two-way switch is in position, it sits neatly clear and over the terminal end of the buzzer. Shorten the point on the brass contact if the clearance is not sufficient between it and the antenna.

*Note:* It is important to ensure that the minimum dimension of $2\frac{5}{8}''$ is available from back of buzzer base to inside of brass battery contacts—otherwise the battery will not fit.

The wiring follows exactly the same circuit as 33D. There are two variations however:

1. The on/off switch is connected between the common connection on the two-way switch and the terminal socket.

128

2. The terminal socket connections now become the brass contact at the base of the antenna and the pointed brass strip contact.

Assuming the two brass battery contacts have been stuck in position, make the longest connections first, keeping the wires tight in the corners of the box. For very short connections, enamelled copper wire can be used, especially where space is limited, from on/off switch to lower tag on antenna.

Have the connecting screws of the on/off switch facing outward and if necessary remove the on/off switch to make it easier.

The sequence of electrical connections is as follows:

1. Common terminal on two-way switch to one side of on/off switch.

2. Opposite terminal of on/off switch to lower brass contact on antenna.

3. Battery contact No. 2 to pointed brass antenna contact.

At this point the box must be re-screwed to the ply rod rest and it is a good idea if it has been painted while work on the box has been done. White on the bank side and a dark colour towards the water is the best combination.

Now the final electrical connections can be made:

4. Battery contact to first buzzer terminal and on to bulb terminal.

5. Second buzzer terminal to one side of two-way switch.

6. Opposite side of two-way switch to other side of bulb holder.

It is wise to make the connections to buzzer and bulb holder before glueing them into position with Araldite.

Most plastic bulb holders are too big for the amount of space we have in the box, and as for the light and buzzer unit previously described, the base will have to be cut off both sides of the terminals. Depending on the size of the buzzer, it may even be necessary to remove the base completely, and the terminals, and solder the connecting wires to the tags left.

Once the bulb holder connections have been made the holder can be glued to the side of the buzzer or the tin whichever is more convenient.

Cement the domed bulb cover into place in the hole in the lid with Plastic Padding, and the unit is ready for testing.

Bend back the tags on a battery and fit it into position. Switch on and move the two-way switch to 'buzzer'. When the antenna adjusting screw is screwed in you should quickly find a point where the buzzer sounds. Turn the screw back a fraction of a turn and the detector is set at its most sensitive point. Move the two-way switch across to 'light' and just touch the antenna. The light should come on.

The two-way switch can be omitted as in the previous unit, so that light and buzzer come on together.

Paint the top of the lid white and the sides of the tin grey.

Using the detector is no different to the head unit described earlier, and Figure 29A on page 108 shows the path the line takes around the antenna. Again it is important to have one rod ring just behind the antenna. The farther the ring is away, the more sensitively the antenna must be set to show a bite, when the baling arm is off.

The only maintenance required is an occasional clean of the brass contacts on antenna, and on the battery with fine glasspaper or emery cloth.

Paint the bank stick the same dark colour as the back of the rod rest.

This book is the result of about five years' fishing and experimenting by the side of one lake, and several rivers in Norfolk. The tackle described has been designed and made either to save money, or to try to outwit a species of fish in its natural environment, when this environment presented particular problems to the angler. Additionally, there is a great sense of satisfaction in actually catching a fish with a piece of tackle made with your own hands.

It is logical therefore, that other waters and species will produce other problems that a gadget, or an adaptation of an old one, will help to solve.

The opportunities are endless, and this book will, I hope, help to stir the ingenuity of many anglers to thinking up, and making, their own equipment.

One man's ideas have always sparked off better ideas in someone else's mind; this is how civilisation has advanced as far as it has today.

Perhaps you, the reader, will find inspiration from only one item from the book and make something better and more efficient.

If you do, this book will have achieved its purpose. That is, always assuming your wife or mother is as patient and understanding as my wife, and is ready to accept that the decorating will not be done while there is a float to make, or a particularly knotty fishing problem that defies a quick answer.

Good fishing and keep your fingers away from the blade.

# Index

NOTE: Asterisk preceding number indicates diagram.

133